Please Change Your Mind

Please Change Your Mind

~

Because You Are What You Think

Steve White

iUniverse, Inc.
Bloomington

Please Change Your Mind
Because You Are What You Think

iUniverse books may be ordered through booksellers or by contacting:

iUniverse
1663 Liberty Drive
Bloomington, IN 47403
www.iuniverse.com
1-800-Authors (1-800-288-4677)

ISBN: 978-1-4620-6690-2 (sc)
ISBN: 978-1-4620-6691-9 (hc)
ISBN: 978-1-4620-6692-6 (e)

Library of Congress Control Number: 2011960419

Printed in the United States of America

iUniverse rev. date: 12/06/2011

For Sherrie, the best person I've ever known,
and to whom I promise all my love, all my life.
And in loving memory of Oboe Charlie and Ginny Lee.

Contents

Preface

I have always been fascinated with the way the mind works. I've read some of Joel Barker's work on vision and paradigms, and some of Stephen Covey's books, particularly *The 7 Habits of Highly Effective People*. I also was exposed to some of the work done by the Franklin Institute in Philadelphia and its Reality Model.

Then I had a meltdown. I thought I was losing my mind. I just couldn't face the world anymore. So I packed up my things, put them in my car, and drove from Atlanta, Georgia, to Coeur d'Alene, Idaho. I left a beautiful wife, a good job, a wonderful house, and disappeared to start life over. I was suffering from clinical depression.

By the time I got there, I knew something was wrong, so I went to the local hospital and spoke to a psychiatrist. I told him my story, and he suggested I check myself into the hospital. It was one of the hardest things I've ever done in my life. I learned that my "running away" was a form of suicide—rather than killing myself, I just made everybody else disappear.

The treatment I received over the next few weeks, in addition to depression medication, was lifesaving. I learned all that I could about cognitive therapy and what is now called CBT, or cognitive behavior therapy. I also read a book by David Burns called *Feeling Good*. The things he described in that book about depression fit me to a T.

My doctor told me at the outset of my treatment that all roads to recovery went through Atlanta. And until I went home and faced the consequences, I would never be truly healed. It was a scary thought, but he was right. I was more than blessed to have a wife and a job that accepted me back. My road to recovery began.

I learned that my mind was the most powerful thing I had. After further study, I came to realize that my cognitions, my thoughts, were the epicenter of control in my life. Everything in my life flowed from my thoughts.

And if that was true, and if I could learn to control my thoughts, then I could control my life. I learned to examine my thoughts on a regular basis, making it a part of my everyday life. Socrates said, "The unexamined life is not worth living." I've come to believe he was right.

And so I began my commitment to forever examine my thoughts. You've probably heard the expression, "Oh, it's all in your mind." Well, it turns out that it really is!

I hope that in reading this book, you will begin to examine your thoughts. I've written it as a layman, because that is all I am. You won't read any scientific terms or complicated formulas. I've tried to put some profound ideas into very simple words. And because a picture is worth a thousand words, I created a graphic that I hope makes it even easier to understand. And it is my prayer that this book will enrich your life.

Steve White

Introduction

All thoughts obviously take place in the mind, and minds are like rear ends—everybody has one. However, few people know the true power of their minds and the power of the things that they think.

Have you ever heard someone say, "Are you out of your mind?" Or, "Have you lost your mind?" We all have. And usually it's after we have said or done something incredibly stupid or incredibly dangerous. Or perhaps it wasn't stupid or dangerous at all, just something out of the norm for most people, which they couldn't identify with it. But a mind isn't something we "lose" or something we're "out of." It is the most powerful controlling force in our life.

The real power of the mind is in our thoughts, or what we think. Someone will say, "I'll have to think about it," or will ask, "What do you think about this?" These types of statements and questions about our thoughts are very close to the power source within each of us, what I call our *Epicenter of Control.*

Bobby Jones had some insight into the power of thoughts when he said, "The game of golf is played on a five-inch course, the distance between your ears." Siddhartha Buddha also understood something of this power when he said, "He is able who thinks he is able." In fact, the mind is so powerful and our thoughts so influential that none of us feel anything, say anything, or do anything without first thinking something. And if that's true, then there is nothing more capable of changing your life than changing your mind.

I confess up front that *Please Change Your Mind* is filled with my personal thoughts and opinions on many things. I make no apology. I share my thoughts only as an example to the reader, not to convince you in any way that my thoughts are right or that yours should change.

So sit back with a glass of wine, read along, and *think!*

1

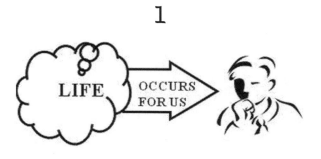

In the Beginning

Life Occurs for Us

Life occurs for each of us every day at one hundred miles per hour. Our lives are so busy, it is hard to keep up with it all. Between our jobs, our families, church, recreation, civic duties, and maybe even a little rest periodically, we process so much information every day that it's a miracle we can function at all.

Technology brings everything on the Internet right to our face, 24/7. Thanks to search engines, social networks, dating services, and much more, we've never had access to more information more conveniently than we have today.

We take all this activity and information in through our five senses. The lion's share of this information gathering is done through seeing and hearing. Our brains or minds (I use these terms interchangeably) are extremely capable, fast computers that process all this life activity in nanoseconds, hundreds of thousands of times each day. No wonder we need sleep.

I have created a graphic diagram that starts in this chapter and builds in subsequent chapters. This diagram will help you follow the logic of the process I will describe.

Each of us has a lens through which we see and process life. All life activity has to pass through that lens before it gets to our brain. In addition to this lens, we all have certain human needs that we are driven to meet.

Human Needs

Psychologists and psychiatrists have written a great deal about basic human needs. Abraham Maslow wrote a paper in 1943 entitled "A Theory of Human Motivation," which proposed a hierarchy of human needs.[1] I believe that Maslow's findings best summarize the collective wisdom of all the experts in regard to human needs. He found that all basic needs could be broken down into five major categories. He believed they were hierarchical, and perhaps they are; but for our purposes I simply agree that they are correct and will refer to them separately. The following pyramid diagram shows Maslow's five basic human needs.

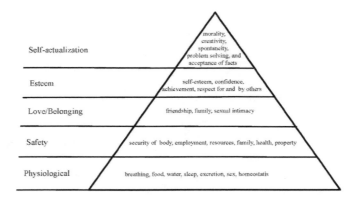

Maslow's Hierarchy of Human Needs

2

Physiological Needs

For the most part, physiological needs are obvious. They are the literal requirements for human survival, the need to live. Air, water, and food are all metabolic requirements for survival in all animals, including humans. Clothing and shelter provide necessary protection from the elements. Human sexual instinct maintains a birth rate sufficient for the survival of the species.

Safety and Security

These needs have to do with our yearning for a predictable, orderly world. These needs include personal security, financial security, health and well-being, and safety nets against accidents and illnesses.

Love and Belonging

We need to feel a sense of belonging and acceptance, whether it comes from large social groups, such as clubs, churches, sports teams, gangs, or professional organizations; or from small, intimate groups. This would include emotionally based relationships in general, such as friends and family. We need to love and be loved by others.

Esteem

We need to be respected and have self-esteem and self-respect. We need to be accepted and valued by others. This would include the need for status, recognition, fame, prestige, and attention. It would also include such things as strength, competency, mastery, self-confidence, independence, and freedom.

Self-Actualization

This need pertains to a person's realizing his or her full potential. It is the desire to become increasingly more of what one is, to become everything that one is capable of being. Individually, this need is specific. In one person it might be a strong desire to become a good parent; in others it might be expressed athletically, or in the arts, or through inventions.

While Maslow's hierarchy of needs has its critics, it is widely accepted. In fact, many courses in marketing and business use his pyramid as one basis for understanding consumers' motives for action. For our purposes in this book, we will look at these needs within individuals, and we will consider them as separate rather than hierarchical.

So our process looks like this:

The *PLEASE CHANGE YOUR MIND* Process

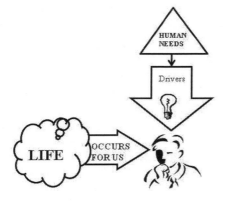

2

The *PLEASE CHANGE YOUR MIND* Process

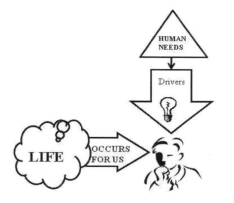

The Lens and the Laws

As stated in the previous chapter, we all have a lens through which we see and process the world and all of life. It is unique to each of us, made obvious by the fact that two people can view the same thing and each see something different. Look at the following picture:[2]

Do you see an old woman? Or do you see a young woman? Look closely and you will see them both. So while you and I can look at the same thing, we may each see something different. But what I see is just as real to me as what you see is real to you. We are looking at the same thing, but the laws we put on our lens could be very different. Similarly, when life comes at us, you and I may witness an event but interpret it differently.

As an example, suppose you and I are on a subway train. We both observe a young boy running through the car unsupervised, while his father sits there and does nothing to control him. You may see a father not disciplining a child and feel angry; I may see a man lost in grief, unable to pay attention to his child, and feel compassion. We both saw the same thing, but because we *thought* something different, we *felt* something different. And if we are both compelled to do something about that boy and his father, then we would certainly *do* something different.

Each of us places our laws on our lens. Laws are the things that you hold to be true. Some of these laws have been placed on your lens by your parents, your teachers, and your friends. But you have put most of them on your lens as you've experienced life, and have come to believe that these laws are true. You have laws on your lens about *everything*. You have hundreds of thousands of laws on your lens, and they filter everything that goes into your brain. You have simple and obvious laws, such as "Fire is hot." But you've also got some complex laws on your lens, like, "My self-worth is dependent on being accepted by my peers." And you have laws of every kind in between those two extremes. You have laws about Dad's way to cut the grass, Mom's way to load the dishwasher. You have laws about marriage, parenting, business, religion, health care, and so forth.

You put these laws in place; you get to approve them before they go on your lens. Mom or Dad may have suggested something was true, but it only goes on your lens with your approval. You adopt these laws largely because you believe they will help you meet one or more of those five human needs.

So you have a lens, and you place on your lens laws that you hold to be true. And then life occurs for you through your lens, in accordance with those laws. It looks something like this:

The *PLEASE CHANGE YOUR MIND* Process

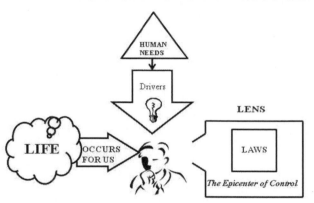

Now let us take a few examples through this process. Let's say you have a law on your lens that says, "All dogs are vicious." What need is probably driving that law? Physiology, or the need to live. Now, when you see a dog, what are you going to feel? Fear. And when you feel fear, what are you likely to do? *Run*, without any doubt.

Notice the progression here. First, something happened—you saw a dog. The next thing you did was think something. You processed seeing that dog through your lens and your law that said "All dogs are vicious." This happens so fast in your mind, you don't even know it. But that is what happens. And it is only after you think something that you feel something, and it is only after you feel something that you do something. This is always the progression. Something happens, you think, you feel, you act. Now our process diagram looks like this:

The *PLEASE CHANGE YOUR MIND* Process

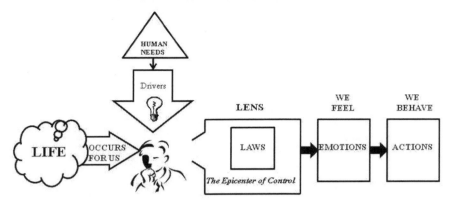

Let's take a few more examples through the process so you get the hang of it. Let's suppose you have a law on your lens that says, "My self-worth is dependent on always being first." Now, what need is probably driving that law? Esteem. You want and need to feel important. So, what will you feel when you start losing in any game? What will you feel when others get credit for something you did? What will you feel in slow traffic? What will you feel in a long line at the bank? You'll feel cheated, you'll feel beaten, you'll feel second class. So if that's what you feel, what will you probably do? Sure, you'll cheat, you'll cut people off, you'll butt in line, and you'll do anything to be first.

Let's take another example. Suppose some of you men out there have a law on your lens that says, "Men are better than women." Not that any man would ever really have this law. Remember, we're just supposing. What need is probably driving a law like that? Esteem again. You need to feel better about yourself. So what will you feel when you get a female boss? What will you feel when your wife makes a decision that you don't agree with? What will you feel about your daughter in relation to your son? Perhaps you'll feel anger toward your boss, perhaps you'll feel resentment toward your wife, and perhaps you'll feel justified in the way you treat your daughter.

If you feel these emotions, what are you then likely to do? You'll find every chance to show up your boss and criticize her. You'll yell at your wife or criticize her, saying she's not capable of making decisions. You'll lay down different rules for your daughter than you have for your son.

Now let's take an example of two women, each with a different law on her lens. Both Mrs. Jones and Mrs. Smith are newlyweds. Mrs. Jones has a law on her lens that says, "If my husband loves me, he'll spend all his time with me on weekends." Mrs. Smith, however, has a law on her lens that says. "My husband will need some time to himself on weekends to decompress from a hard week at work."

Now comes Saturday morning. Both Mrs. Jones and Mrs. Smith have gotten up early to fix breakfast for their husbands, probably because they also have a law on their lens that says something like, "Cooking breakfast is a good way to show my husband that I love him." Then down the stairs come Mr. Jones and Mr. Smith with their golf clubs slung over their shoulders, and they both say, "I'm off to play golf, honey."

What do you think Mrs. Jones is going to feel? She's going to feel anger, and probably hurt as well. The human need she's trying to fulfill is love. She needs to feel loved, and if her husband loved her, he'd spend the weekend with her. Since Mrs. Jones feels anger, what is she likely to do? Of course, she's going to yell and scream, or maybe sulk.

Now, what is Mrs. Smith likely to feel? She will probably feel compassion, because her law says that her husband will need time alone on weekends to decompress. So what do think Mrs. Smith is going to do? Of course, she's going to give her husband a kiss and tell him to have a great time with his buddies.

In this example, both Mrs. Jones and Mrs. Smith observed the exact same event. Both husbands came down the stairs with the golf clubs over their shoulders and said the exact same thing. The only thing that was different was the *law* on each woman's lens. That law dictated what each woman felt and did. What do you think the results in real life would have been? Which woman's actions probably generated the result that is most likely to meet her needs?

Now I'm not here to tell you that the laws on your lens are good or bad. I'm just saying that you *have* a lens, and that you are *putting* laws on that lens every day. Those laws are dictating what you *feel,* and your feelings are then dictating what you *do.* And what you do is creating the results in your life.

3

The *PLEASE CHANGE YOUR MIND* Process

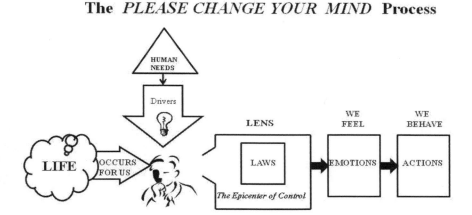

The Results We Create for Ourselves

So now you've seen that when life occurs for you every day, at one hundred miles per hour, you process all of life through your lens. On that lens are the laws that you hold to be true, and they have all been placed there by you, with your permission. When life meets those laws, you instantaneously think something that is based on those laws. This, in turn, causes you to feel an emotion, like anger or compassion. These feelings, or emotions, then dictate what you do. It is always this progression—something happens, you think, you feel, you act, and you create results.

Our diagram now looks like this:

The *PLEASE CHANGE YOUR MIND* Process

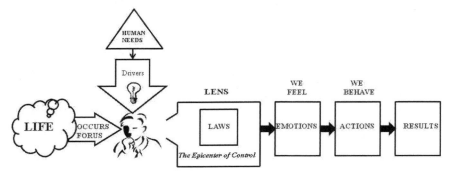

The results that you produce in your life provide feedback to the mind. This feedback, positive or negative, is always being measured (subconsciously) against your five basic human needs. When there is harmony between your results and your needs, you have a sense of satisfaction, well-being, and peace. When your results don't produce harmony with your needs, you end up in conflict, dissatisfied, without peace, and the sense that something is wrong. So now our diagram is complete and looks like this:

The *PLEASE CHANGE YOUR MIND* Process

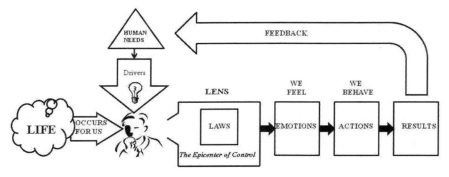

Let's say that there is some aspect of your life that is not meeting your needs. You have no peace and you know something needs to change. How do you fix it? Well, there are a thousand books that will tell you to change your behavior. And there are another thousand books that will tell you that since you can't change what happens in life, you should change the way that you feel about life. But I believe that while focusing on your behavior and your feelings might provide some short-term benefit, it will never produce long-term peace.

It is very frustrating to try to change your behavior or your emotions if you keep the same laws on your lens. Those laws drive the other two. To make lasting positive changes, so that the results of your actions lead to long-term peace, you have to alter the laws. If you can do that, you will automatically change the way you feel, change what you do, and create different results. While the new results may still not meet your needs, they will produce something different from before.

For example, if someone has a law on his lens that says, "Men are better than women," and he changes it to, "Women are better than men," the results probably still won't meet his needs. So he keeps changing the laws! Sooner or later maybe he'll hit upon, "Men and women are equal," and he will experience the peace he was looking for.

Said another way, if the results of your behavior are not meeting your needs over time, you have an unsuitable law on your lens. Let me repeat that. *If the results of your behavior are not meeting your needs over time, you have an unsuitable law on your lens.*

I believe that all human growth is the result of people changing the laws on their lenses. If you can take a law off your lens, put it on the table, examine it, and have the courage to change it and then put it back, you have the formula for producing results in your life that will meet your needs.

You must always remember that results take time to measure. If a teenager has a law on her lens that says, "My self-worth is dependent on being accepted by my friends," and she goes to parties where drugs and alcohol are being served, what will she feel? She will feel pressure, and she will feel that her friends' acceptance is slipping away. So what will she do? Sure, she'll take the drugs and drink the alcohol. Now, is that going to meet her needs over time? Of course not. But it will provide her with some short-term benefit.

But what if we could get that same teenager to change the law on her lens to: "Drugs and alcohol are bad for me, not to mention against the law, so even though I want to be accepted, I'm not going to do drugs and alcohol"? What result would be created? The immediate result might be short-term pain resulting from ridicule from her friends. But remember, *results take time to measure!* And I'll bet that if you could ask that same girl at age twenty-five how that new law is working out for her, she would probably agree that the results she's producing are meeting her needs, and she is at peace.

Of all the laws that people put on their lenses, the ones that are the most damaging are the ones relating to a person's self-worth. Your self-worth is determined by you. It is totally internal. Nobody can make you feel inferior without your permission. When a person's self-worth is tied to anything external, his or her needs will not be met over time. How many people do you know whose self-worth is tied up in something external—their job, wardrobe, education, club/gang, salary, winning, possessions, and so forth? The list goes on and on. Trying to bolster self-worth through such externals often leads to depression and other problems.

Look at the diagram below.[3]

ROLES

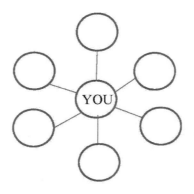

The center circle is you, the core essence of who you really are. The outer circles represent the different roles you have in life. Put one of your roles in each of the circles. It may be spouse, parent, teacher, coach, Boy Scout leader, Sunday school teacher, tennis player, etc. When you have at least five or six roles, rate how good you are in each of your roles. On a scale of one to ten, where ten is best, how do you rate yourself in each of your roles?

Okay, now rate the center circle, the deep inner you, the core essence of who you are as a human being, using the same scale. Maybe you rated yourself an eight as a spouse, or maybe a nine as a parent, or even a ten as Little League coach or Girl Scout leader. But what did you rate yourself in the center circle?

This is where self-worth becomes critical. Research shows that you can never perform higher in any outer circle than you consider yourself to be in the center circle. *Never let your self-worth be dependent on anything external.* It is a personal and internal determination. Based on your assessment of the results you're creating in your life today, if you suspect you have a law on your lens that bases your self-worth on anything external, you should reevaluate that law today.

4

The *PLEASE CHANGE YOUR MIND* Process

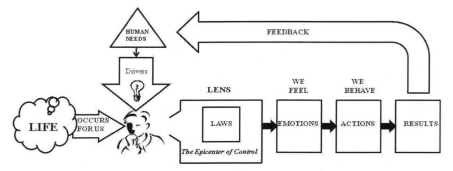

Using the Process Diagram

Let's just review what we have learned up to this point:

- Life occurs for all of us at one hundred mph.
- You have five basic human needs that you're trying to meet.
- You have a lens through which you process life.
- You have laws on your lens, which contain all the things that you hold to be true.
- Nothing goes on your lens without your permission. You totally control it.
- When life happens, your laws dictate what you think.
- What you think drives an emotion that makes you feel.
- What you feel drives your actions and behavior, or what you do.
- What you do creates results in your life.

- This progression is always the same—something happens, you think, you feel, you act, and you create results.
- Results provide feedback to your mind.
- If your results meet your needs over time, you will experience peace.
- If your results do not meet your needs over time, you probably have a bad law on your lens.
- Results take time to measure.
- All human growth is the process of changing the laws on our lenses.
- If your self-worth is dependent on anything external, you have a problem.
- The Epicenter of Control is your thoughts—the laws on your lens.

So you might rightfully ask, "How do I use this process diagram?" The first thing you have to do is examine the various aspects of your life and see if anything appears broken. Are there problem areas where you know your needs are not being met and you're not at peace? Perhaps it's your marriage, perhaps it's a rebellious teenager, perhaps it's your job, perhaps it's your spiritual life. It could be anything.

Behavior

Once you have determined there is a problem area, you need to look at your behavior patterns. You basically work your way backward through the process diagram. You start with what you know is a problem area, because your needs are not being met. Then the only thing you really have to look at is your behavior. Do you see any patterns? Do you see any repeated behavior that you don't like?

Emotions and Needs

Once you have identified a behavior pattern that you don't like, then you need to see what needs might be driving such behavior. It is also helpful to reflect on what you were feeling just before you acted. Since our feelings drive our behavior and actions, there is always a correlation. Identifying the emotion that drives the behavior is the key.

Laws

After you have identified either the possible need or emotion that drove the behavior, try to determine what law could be on your lens that would make you feel and act that way. There may be more than one law at play, and there may be more than one need governing your thoughts. If possible, try to identify alternative laws that you could consider. Put the new law on your lens and try it out in real life.

When you are interacting with other people, it is often helpful to evaluate their behavior. Many times you will gain insight into what they are feeling or what need they're trying to meet. If you can identify a need or emotion, you might be able to determine some of the laws on their lenses that are creating that behavior. Once you can do this, predicting another person's behavior becomes easier. It can even lead to a discussion about that person's lens and laws.

One of the great aspects of the lens-and-laws language is that it allows you to have conversations with other people that are nonthreatening. Take my son, for example. When Sean was a teenager, he began hanging around with a couple of boys I didn't particularly care for. Whenever he went out with these boys, there always seemed to be trouble. But instead of just confronting him and telling him how bad I thought his behavior was, I was able to approach him with the language of the process diagram. I could say to him, "Hey, Sean, can I talk to you? I think you might have a bad law on your lens. Now you're fine, but I think maybe we should explore some of the laws on your lens."

That approach immediately took personality out of the discussion. There was nothing wrong with him; his lens and laws were the problem. It immediately depersonalized the situation, and we were able to examine it rationally and without raising our voices. As it turned out, Sean had a self-worth law that was tied to acceptance by his peers, and he was eventually able to replace it. If you can get the whole family using the language of the diagram, it will become an amazing tool.

In closing this chapter, I would like to repeat that you have hundreds of thousands of laws on your lens, which you use in every aspect of your life. In fact, there is no aspect of anyone's life that isn't driven by the laws on his or her lens.

In the chapters ahead we will look at some different aspects of life; and using the *Please Change Your Mind* process diagram, we will explore some solutions to common problems that we all face.

5

The *PLEASE CHANGE YOUR MIND* Process

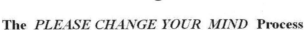

Some Everyday Examples

I want to look at some everyday examples and use the process diagram for some common laws that might be on the lens of someone you know (not you, of course). Let's start with a simple one that I grew up with—"Men don't cry." Do you know anyone with that law on his (or her) lens? My dad had that law on his lens, and as a result, I grew up with it. Eventually I put that law on my lens too. So what need could drive a law like that? Maybe self-esteem or self-actualization.

So with that law, what will a man do at a funeral? What will he do when he is overwhelmed with joy? That's right—he'll stifle it or repress it. What is he likely to feel then? Embarrassment, or maybe even feel like less than a man. So if that is what he feels, what is he likely to do? He'll try to hide it. He'll turn his head away, and maybe even leave the room. Now take it a step further. What if instead of a man, this was a little boy? What will he feel when he falls down and skins his knee? He certainly won't feel that he can cry, especially if Dad is around. It's a shame that some people just won't give men and boys permission to cry.

Let's turn the situation around a little. What if *Mom* has this law on her lens? What will she feel if her husband or young son ever cries? She, too, will probably feel embarrassment and maybe even anger. What might she do? She might ridicule them in front of others or yell at her son, "Grow up, Johnny, and be a man." All of these thoughts, feelings, and actions are really rather predictable if you know the law on the lens.

Self-Worth

So, what about this one—"My self-worth is dependent on my possessions"? What kind of need drives a law like that? Sure, the need to feel important. So what type of car do you think this person will drive? What kind of neighborhood do you think he or she will live in? What kind of wardrobe will he or she have, what kind of watch?, What kind of shoes will he or she buy?

There is a very similar law that says, "My job defines who I am." Will this person ever be happy in a blue-collar job? What kind of things, even illegal or unethical things, might this person be willing to do to keep his or her job? I saw a TV show the other night in which the man was a commodities trader on Wall Street. He had a wife and two little boys, was involved in community and civic activities, and was admired by friends and neighbors. He also had the law on his lens that said, "My self-worth is dependent on my possessions." So he bought a new house, two new cars, and incurred significant debt. Within a few months, his business went south, and suddenly he didn't have enough money to pay the bills.

He lost his job, but he didn't tell his wife. Instead, he left home every day at the same time and told his family he was going to work. Why? Because his self-worth was tied to that job. After a few months, the savings account was empty, the college fund was depleted, and he became desperate. Guess what he decided to do? What would you have done?

He decided that the best option available to him was to rob banks! Can you believe it? Why? His self-worth was tied to those possessions, and he couldn't bring himself to part with them. Now he's in jail, his wife divorced him, and he can't see his kids. Do you think these results are going to meet his needs over time? Robbing banks met his needs for a couple of months, until he got caught. Remember, results take time to measure.

Executives

Sue was an executive at a large company. She had been with the company for over twenty-five years and had risen close to the top of the corporate ladder. She started to develop some health problems, and her husband thought it was stress related. As her conditioned worsened, she decided to approach management and seek a lower, less stressful position. The company was very understanding and granted her request.

This decision resulted in a significant decrease in pay, but Sue had successfully changed the law on her lens from, "I want to be promoted and make more money," to "My health is more important than my salary." And yet I know another businesswoman who has a law on her lens that says, "My job defines me as a person." And while she has health problems as well, she will never consider a lower position. Her self-worth is too tightly connected to her job.

Entitlement

One of the things that seems to be prevalent in our society today is a sense of entitlement. Many people apparently have a law on their lens that says, "I'm entitled."

I remember after Hurricane Katrina how so many people were outraged that the federal government wasn't there the next day with food, clothing, shelter, water, and money! And, worse than that, they felt entitled to it. It was a law that was (is) on the lens of a whole group of people.

In contrast to the "I'm entitled" mentality is the mind-set that "I'm responsible for taking care of me." There was a category-five snowstorm in Montana, the Dakotas, and Wyoming in October 2005, less than two months after Hurricane Katrina hit. Twenty-four inches of snow fell, and winds were up to fifty miles per hour. Roads were closed, people lost power and had no heat, they couldn't get to the store to buy food or prescriptions drugs, and motorists were stranded. The governor of North Dakota declared a state of emergency. But there was no public outrage expressed by the people, demanding federal government assistance.

When you contrast the people's response in New Orleans to the people's response in the North, it demonstrates the difference between the laws of "I'm entitled" and "I'm responsible for taking care of me."

I think the same is probably true of some welfare recipients. Some people are now third-generation welfare recipients and probably have come to feel entitled.[4] So, with the law of "I'm entitled" on your lens, you will feel "entitled" in every situation where you require some kind of help. And when you feel entitled, you don't ask for help, you demand it.

What will happen when these people's entitlements are taken away? They'll be outraged. They'll feel like they've lost a God-given right. So, what are they likely to do? They'll protest, they'll riot, they'll demand, and they may even try to take back what was taken from them.

Not all people on government entitlement programs feel entitled. Many perceived that they needed a hand up, not a handout. Many women who have been on welfare have taken advantage of education programs, gotten good jobs, and come off the welfare rolls. They are to be applauded for their efforts.

Bullying

Another common problem in society today is bullying. Most bullies probably have a law on their lenses that says, "I feel better about myself when I put you down." The need driving this is to feel important. So when a vulnerable peer comes along, they think, "I'll feel better about myself if I can humiliate you, denigrate you, or hurt you." They feel empowered and proceed to bully the other person. Is this behavior going to create results that will meet their needs over time? Let's hope not.

But let me say a word to those who might be victims of bullying. You do *not* have to take it! Whenever you feel bullied, you should report it to a teacher or your parents, and in some extreme cases, even the police.

Just as important as reporting bullying is, you need to put a law on your lens that says, "No one can make me feel inferior without my permission." You are special, and anybody that tries to tell you otherwise is just wrong. I saw a kid being bullied once at a Little League game. The boy turned to the bully and said, "You're so lame," and then walked away. It was powerful. The boy just refused to be bullied, and you can too.

Boys vs. Girls

Another thing that I see a lot in younger kids is a double standard for acceptable activities. It seems to be okay for a little girl to do "boy" things. She gets called a tomboy, but that seems to have no significant social stigma. But many people seem to have a law on their lenses that says, "If a little boy does girl things, then he's a sissy." So what do you think when you see a boy playing with a doll? Yep, sissy. What do you then feel? Perhaps you feel offended, or angry. A dad who thinks that men shouldn't cry will probably yell at the boy and take the doll away.

This can carry over to adulthood. I knew a man who had a law on his lens that said, "Men don't cook, it's a girly thing." So when his son wanted to become a chef, do you think the father was supportive? Of course not.

Getting Old

Many of us have laws even about aging. George Burns said that if he'd known he was going to live so long, he'd have taken better care of himself. But women seem especially sensitive about their age. Actually, I don't think it is their actual age that bothers them; it's looking old at any age that they don't like. And as I tell my wife, "Being a grandfather isn't so bad. It's being married to a grandmother that bugs me!"

All kidding aside, how many women have a law on their lenses that says, "My husband won't love me if I look old," or "I'll never find a husband at my age," or, "My self-worth is dependent on how I look"? Have you ever met anyone who had a law like that? Me either. But just imagine what goes through a woman's mind every time she looks in a mirror if she has laws like that. She'll feel terrible about herself.

So what will she do? Just about anything. Certainly plastic surgery—tummy tucks, face-lifts, breast implants, tanning beds, etc. I make sure my wife knows I love her regardless of how she looks and how old we get. After all, I'm no spring chicken either. So men, make your women feel secure, and don't let them go around with laws that will never meet their needs over time. Remember, nobody has ever won the war against old age.

Driving

What about driving a car? Do you know anybody who goes through a personality transformation when he or she gets behind the wheel? What kind of law is on the lens of somebody who engages in road rage? Research shows that the major causes of road rage are traffic congestion, time constraints, and people who are distracted. Road-ragers might also feel that they are targets of malicious acts, and have a sense of entitlement and a sense of self-righteousness.

Somehow these causes have manifested themselves as laws, which have found their way onto the lenses of many drivers. This causes them to feel anger. They act out by cutting people off, giving them the finger, tailgating, and in the worst of cases, even dueling with another car. Drivers can become physically violent if they stop. Another major cause of anger among drivers is people using cell phones, either to talk or text or even check their e-mail while driving, and not paying enough attention to the road. Unfortunately, the number of incidents of road rage is increasing every year.

Saving

What about the couple who thinks, "We can't save, we need all our money just to live"? Is that going to meet their needs over time? One of the greatest gifts you can give your children is the habit of saving. Pay yourself first. Put 10 percent away before you do anything else. One day you will want to retire, and the money will be there. The federal government has already spent all its money, along with another $14 trillion it borrowed. Don't be like the government! Save regularly and don't depend on Social Security. I don't care what your income is. You can always find a way to get by on 10 percent less, so do it today.

The Big Shot

When I was in high school, I was a pretty popular guy. I played football, basketball, and baseball, and I was the captain of the baseball team. I was a pretty handsome guy, too, and I dated the prettiest girl in the school. I had a pretty hot ride—a white 1958 Chevy with a 348 engine, three deuce carburetors, and a white rolled and pleated interior, with four on the floor.

As a result of all this, most of the kids in the school knew who I was. I got a lot of attention, and over time, I began to consider myself a big shot. I saw that I always got special attention just because of who I was. Not unpredictably, I put a law on my lens that said, "Big shots like me have a different set of rules." Or alternately stated, "No rules apply to me because I'm a big shot."

You can probably guess that the need driving this was self-esteem and the desire to feel important. So with that law, whenever someone told me what the rule was about anything, I felt offended. Rules weren't for me. Didn't they know I was a big shot? So what do you suppose I did? I broke all the rules because I was a big shot.

So by breaking all the rules, what kind of results do you think I created for myself? Do you think they met my needs? You bet they did! But would they meet my needs over time? No way.

My high school baseball coach, who thought I had major league potential, was the first to spot my problem. He asked me one day why I thought the world revolved around me. "What do you mean?" I asked him. He told me he'd seen that I never wanted to do the drills that all my other teammates did. Then he told me that when I went to college, or perhaps even to the big leagues, I was going to be seen as just an average guy, not the superstar I was in high school.

He told me to practice hard like all the other guys, because he wasn't going to have special rules just for me. It was a rude awakening, but I changed my law that day. So far, the results are meeting my needs.

My coach didn't focus on my behavior, but on my attitude. My old law had affected many areas of my life, like homework, school attendance, chores, curfews, drinking, smoking, and on and on. Once I changed my law, my behavior changed by itself.

The Pilot

I have a friend who is a pilot with a major airline. He's been flying with the company for over twelve years. Every so often the pilots have to do simulator testing to keep their skills sharp, and they get tested in emergency situations that rarely happen in normal flying. My friend has what is called test anxiety, and he has never done well on tests.

Recently he had to go in for his regularly scheduled simulator testing. At that time, his wife was having health problems of an unknown origin. He was nervous, worried, and filled with negative thoughts. He didn't do well and had to go before a review board. I had lunch with him soon after and we discussed his situation. I told him I was writing a book, and I explained a little about what it was about.

I suggested to him that perhaps he'd had a law on his lens for many years that said, "I don't do well in simulators." I suggested that he examine the possibility that he had such a law and to consider changing it to, "I do my best work in simulators." He'll be tested again soon, and I'll let you know how he does in my next book.

Conclusion

Fortunately, there are many more good laws on your lens than bad ones. Good laws like "It always pays to be polite and courteous" will definitely meet your needs over time. The bad laws, however, tend not to meet your needs. Laws like "All Muslims are terrorists," "Whites are better than blacks" (unfortunately still held true today by the Ku Klux Klan and others), "All immigrants are here illegally." These are what I call hasty generalizations, and they paint a whole group with the same brush. But these laws do exist on the lenses of some of the people that we meet every day.

So if your needs are not being met over time, there is probably a bad law on your lens. Have the courage to take it down, examine it, and change it to something that might work better for you and might start meeting your needs. To quote Socrates again, "The unexamined life is not worth living." So start examining your life. What can it hurt, right?

6

Businesses Have Laws Too

There are many companies out there today with laws on their corporate lenses that are not meeting their needs. First let's look at a few major companies, before we get to some individual specifics.

Swiss Watchmakers

In the late 1960s, the Swiss owned about 80 percent of the world watch market. Ten years later, 80 percent of the world's watch market belonged to the Japanese. What happened? The quartz crystal. But I bet you would be surprised to learn who invented the quartz crystal. Swiss researchers did! But when they took the idea to management, management said, "There are no gears or mainsprings. This can't possibly be the future of watches." They were so sure of this conclusion, they didn't even protect the idea. Later that year, the Swiss displayed their invention to the world. The Japanese took one look, and ten years later they had taken over the international watch market. The Swiss watchmakers had a law on their lens that said, "All watches have gears and mainsprings." This law was so powerful that they were blinded to an opportunity that represented the future of watches.

Another subtle law was at play here. What was the business case for the Swiss? They had invested heavily in building manufacturing plants for gears and mainsprings. If the quartz crystal was the future, they would have to walk away from their investment in gears and mainsprings, and reinvest in manufacturing quartz crystals. This could not have been an appealing option. The Japanese, on the other hand, had no such investment in gears and mainsprings; therefore, their business case had to look much more attractive. Sometimes you have to be willing to walk away from all that you are in order to become all that you can be. The Swiss concluded that they couldn't afford to do it, when really they couldn't afford *not* to do it.

Enron and Arthur Andersen

Enron was an energy company formed in 1985 by Kenneth Lay. After Jeffrey Skilling was hired as president, Enron grew to a $63 billion company. Skilling developed a staff of executives that, through a series of accounting loopholes, special purpose entities, and poor financial reporting, was able to hide billions in debt from failed deals and projects. Chief Financial Officer Andrew Fastow and others misled the Enron board of directors and audit committee on high-risk accounting practices and pressured Arthur Andersen, their auditor, to ignore the issues.

In the end, Enron shareholders lost nearly $11 billion when Enron's stock price fell from ninety dollars per share in mid-2000, to less than one dollar per share in November 2001. The US Securities and Exchange Commission (SEC) began an investigation, and in December 2001 Enron filed bankruptcy under Chapter 11, which made it the largest corporate bankruptcy in United States history (until WorldCom's bankruptcy in 2002). Enron employees also lost billions in pensions and 401(k) plans.

Many executives at Enron were indicted on a variety of charges and were later sentenced to prison. Arthur Andersen was also found guilty in a US District Court. While Andersen's conviction was later overturned by the US Supreme Court, the firm had already lost the majority of its customers and had shut down its operations.

As a consequence of the scandal, new regulations and legislation were enacted to expand the accuracy of financial reporting for public companies. One primary piece of legislation was the Sarbanes-Oxley Act, which expanded the repercussions for destroying, altering, or fabricating records in federal investigations, or for attempting to defraud shareholders. It also increased the accountability of auditing firms to remain unbiased and independent of their clients.

So the executives of Enron, collectively, had laws on their lenses that said, "Borderline accounting principles are okay," and "Hiding our activities from the board is okay," and "Coercing our auditor to be complicit with us is okay." As a result of these laws, the executives felt insulated and safe from any repercussions. Their deception met their needs for a while, but results take time to measure. In the end, many of them went to jail.

The partners at Arthur Andersen were equally guilty and had some laws on their lenses that were equally bad. Andersen was accused of reckless standards in their audits, as well as conflict of interest. While Andersen received annual audit fees of $25 million from Enron, it also received annual consulting fees of $27 million. The firm was accused of concealing the actual financials in order to continue receiving the annual consulting fees. When news of the SEC investigation of Enron was made public, Andersen attempted to cover up any negligence by shredding several tons of documents and deleting nearly fifty thousand e-mails from its computer systems.

The executives at Arthur Andersen had laws on their lenses that said, "It's okay to help our clients defraud their shareholders" and "If we get caught, it's okay to cover-up." These laws also met their needs for a short time. But in the end, the company went out of business, leaving thousands without jobs. They had broken the public trust. Most Fortune 500 companies that used Andersen fired them, and who can blame them. Rarely has a company the size of Andersen fallen so quickly, and all because of a few laws on the lenses of a few people.

Railroads

One of the first chartered railroads in the United States was the Baltimore and Ohio (B&O) founded in 1827. Authorized by the Pacific Railway Act of 1862, it was the first transcontinental railway and one of the crowning achievements of President Abraham Lincoln, completed four years after his death. The railroad business grew and had its largest impact on America during the second half of the nineteenth century. Railroads at that time seemed indispensible to the development of a national America. From 1900 to 1950, the expansion of railroads included growth in passengers as well as freight.

In the early 1930s, the automobile began to compete with the railroads for passenger traffic. By the 1950s, the Interstate Highway System was emerging, as well as commercial aviation. On the freight side, trucking was becoming a major competitor to railroads. The final blow for railroads was the loss of railroad post offices in the 1960s. Labor unions and overregulation also had an impact on the rail industry.

Through all the rise and fall of railroads, I suspect that there was one constant law on their lens. And that law said, "We're in the railroad business," when in fact, they were in the transportation business. Railroad companies never invested in the auto industry or the airline industry or the cargo ship industry, even as those industries were growing up around them at the peak of the railroad business. Probably the railroad companies felt that railroads would be there forever and the sky was the limit. That met their needs for a while. But results take time to measure, and as Paul Harvey would say, "And now you know the rest of the story."

IBM

International Business Machines was my first job. I went to work for the company right out of school and learned to become a computer programmer. I worked for IBM for about five years, and then I left to get into the banking industry on the technology side. While I was only with IBM a short time, I had a tremendous respect for the company. It paved the way in the computer industry, and yet it had two bad laws on its corporate lens.

IBM started out as an office equipment company and made thousands of typewriters in the 1940s. Tom Watson, the founder, had a vision of the future, but for all the wonderful things IBM created in its research labs, there was one opportunity it completely missed. A man named Chester Carlson, a patent attorney, developed a process called electrophotography. He tried for ten years to get a company to buy into his idea, but with no luck. He took his idea to IBM, and IBM turned him down. I should note that other companies like Kodak, General Electric, and RCA also looked at the idea and turned him down. Finally, the Battelle Memorial Institute, a non-profit organization, invested in Chester Carlson's idea. Battelle then signed a licensing agreement with a company called Haloid. Batelle and Haloid collaborated in research and demonstrated electrophotography in 1948. Haloid subsequently became the Xerox Corporation.

Carlson's process is now known as xerography, and there probably is not an office in the world today without a copy machine, laser printer, or fax machine. IBM and the other companies had laws on their lenses that simply blinded them to the opportunity.

Interestingly, the other IBM misstep involved computers. IBM is considered the father company of all computers. But it missed the concept of the personal computer. The law on its lens was, apparently, "Computers aren't affordable by the masses." IBM saw the computer as something businesses needed, but not necessarily individuals. It did enter the game, but late. Further, IBM really had no experience in the retail market, and the margins, due to significant competition, were thin. IBM eventually sold its PC division in 2004 to a Chinese firm in Beijing called Lenova Group, for $1.75 billion.

Other Laws in Business

In the movie *Field of Dreams,* Kevin Costner hears a voice that repeatedly says, "If you build it, they will come." Well, it worked for a baseball field in Iowa, but it doesn't always work in business. Many manufacturers have had this same law on their lenses, and it is never a foregone conclusion that anyone *will* come. Many a company has believed that law and overbuilt its supply, only to find there was no demand. That law didn't meet their needs for very long.

Businesses develop a culture with corporate laws. How about the law that says, "Our products won't sell in Europe"? And because of that, they never *try* to take their product to Europe. Or how about this one: "We'll make it up in volume"? Well, what if you don't? A sound business plan determines if high entry costs can be overcome by large volume sales.

There are some other good ones, like, "Good customer service will bring our customers back." If that law could be instilled in the company culture, it would drive what people did every day. Nothing would ever go wrong that couldn't be fixed to the customer's satisfaction.

An extension of the Enron law is, "It's okay to cheat a little on taxes." Or how about, "We try to pay our people as little as possible to keep our expenses down"? Is that going to meet a company's needs? No way. With that law, a high turnover rate is virtually guaranteed. There are hundreds more, like, "My boss hates me." What need might be driving a law like that? What is the employee going to feel every time his or her boss asks him or her to do something? What is he or she most likely to do? Do you think the results of his or her actions are going to meet his or her needs over time?

One of the best books I ever read was written by Napoleon Hill in 1928, called *The Law of Success.* In the book he discusses sixteen specific laws related to both personal and business success:

- Definite purpose—know where you're going
- Mastermind alliance—seek cooperation from others
- Applied faith—believe in yourself, put fear behind you
- Go the extra mile—provide more and better service than you are paid for
- Pleasing personality—courtesy and a positive mental attitude
- Personal initiative—get busy, don't procrastinate
- Positive mental attitude—the most important component of success
- Enthusiasm—it inspires action and is contagious
- Self-discipline—ties all the other laws together
- Accurate thinking—separating fact from fiction, and the important from the unimportant
- Controlled action—keep your mind *on* what you want and *off* what you don't want
- Teamwork—cooperation from others is essential
- Adversity and defeat—you are never a failure until you accept defeat as permanent and quit trying
- Creative vision—sees no limitations
- Maintenance of sound health—anything that affects your physical health, affects your mental health
- Budgeting time and money—take regular inventory to see you're spending both

Hill's book is nearly 1,200 pages long, so he obviously wrote much about each of these laws for success. Whatever laws you have on your lens about what it takes to be a success, consider changing them to these laws. The book is a wonderful read, and it will empower you.

Let me close this chapter with a story about identical twin brothers. They went to the same schools, took the same classes, and graduated at the same time with the same degree. Each started his own company, making the exact same product. Just before it was time to go to market, they each had to decide what color the product should be. The first brother said, "Paint it blue!" The second brother wanted to make sure he got this right, so he hired a research firm to interview consumers about the best color. In three months the consultants came back and said, "Research shows conclusively that the product should be painted red." So, the second brother painted all his product red. When he finally put his product on the market, he found that nobody wanted it. Everyone already had a blue one.

Now there are a couple of morals to this story. One is that sometimes any decision is better than no decision. But I bet the first brother had a law on his lens that said, "The first to market usually wins." That drove what he thought, what he felt, and what he did. The results would seem to have met his needs.

7

Oh Baby, Will You Marry Me?

Many people will tell you that the key to a happy and successful marriage is communication. That may be true, but there are other significant factors that come into play, like trust and commitment. When I married my wife Sherrie twenty-seven years ago, we both had two children from a previous marriage. We each had a boy and a girl, and we each had custody of our children. When we married, we put four teenagers together in the same house. It was not the Brady Bunch.

Marriage is tough enough without complicating it with stepchildren. But Sherrie and I had been married to our ex-spouses for seventeen or eighteen years, and we drew a lot of experience from our first marriages. We knew that putting two families together would be a chore. So in addition to the traditional marriage vows, Sherrie and I wrote our own vows of what we wanted to promise to each other. The first was, "We will love and treat each other's children as our own." Boy, am I ever glad we promised that! Teenagers are a challenge at the best of times, and having step-teenagers seemed like a death wish. If her kids liked Cheerios, mine liked Corn Flakes; and if her kids liked Colgate, mine liked Crest.

I'm thankful to report today that we all survived, and we have eight wonderful grandchildren. In fact, I would go so far as to say that my son and Sherrie's daughter are closer with each other now than they are to their biological siblings. And that is a testament to them more than to us.

The second vow we promised was, "No problem will ever be bigger than our lifelong commitment to each other." No marriage is without problems. Sherrie and I knew that because we were both divorced, which clearly indicates that some problems had been bigger than our commitment to our ex-spouses. So we knew problems would come. We just promised each other that we were committed to working through all of them, whatever they were.

These were the two laws we put on our lenses on our wedding day, and I have to tell you that the results have met our needs over time. But there was one other promise Sherrie made to me. She said, "If you ever hit me, don't go to sleep." I've never hit her!

I have learned over the years that Sherrie has some unique laws on her lens that say, "Toilet seats are always to be down, beds are always to be made, and dishes are either to be put in the cupboard or in the dishwasher." I have no idea when she put these laws on her lens, but by golly, I know they're there. If I get up in the middle of the night to go to the bathroom, when I come back, Sherrie has made the bed. When I get back in bed, she goes in the bathroom to put the toilet seat back down and checks to see if I left a glass in the sink!

Maybe I'm exaggerating a bit. But I have come to accept the fact that she has these laws, and she has come to accept the fact that I don't. It's working out well so far.

One last thing I have to tell you about Sherrie is the way she gives directions. I don't know whether this is a law on her lens or whether she is just directionally challenged. Some of you men out there might see this phenomenon in other members of the female gender. When Sherrie gives directions, she never uses east, west, north, or south, and she never uses distances. And she spends as much time telling you where you aren't as she does telling you where you are. For example, she'll say, "Go down the road until you get to the house with the green mailbox. That's not it. Keep going. When you reach the McDonald's on your right, you're almost there. At the next stop sign, turn left. I don't know the name of the road." And I still love her.

Okay, just one more thing I'd like to share about Sherrie. This, too, may be prevalent among others of her gender. Sherrie never answers the question you ask her. Ever notice how some people do that? When I ask her, "How long until dinner is ready?", she'll say, "I'm taking up the potatoes now." Or when we're going out I'll ask, "Honey, how long until you're ready to go?" And she'll say, "I'm putting on my lipstick now." She never answers with a measurement of time; instead she tells me what she's doing. If I ask her if she'd like to go out for dinner that night, expecting one of two possible answers, yes or no, she'll say, "Well, I took some chicken out of the freezer." Ninety percent of the time she doesn't answer the question I ask her. And I still love her.

I've heard a story about a couple who went to see a marriage counselor. Once they had exchanged pleasantries, the counselor turned to the man and asked, "What seems to be the matter?' The man responded, "I just don't love her anymore." To which the counselor replied, "Well, that's the problem. Go home and love her." For too many people, the law on their lens is that love is a noun, something we feel, or something you're in. But love is a *verb*. It is something you do!

When my younger daughter got married, I gave a little toast at the reception, and I gave her and my son-in-law some advice. I told them to say or do something every day that made the other one feel cherished. That is making love a verb. Sherrie lets me know I'm loved in virtually everything she does. That is love as a verb.

I believe one of the biggest problems in marriage today is the lack of communication. If there is a problem, it needs to be discussed. I've known women who, when they get offended by something, will pout and give their husbands the silent treatment. Finally, when a man asks his wife what's wrong, she'll say, "Nothing." Then he'll say, "I can tell by the way you're acting that something is wrong." Her response? "Well, if I have to tell you, then never mind!"

Does this sound familiar? Know anyone who has had that experience? When problems arise, put the snake on the table and talk about it. It does no good to keep it hidden. When something bothers you, discuss it with your mate.

Many people are just too nonconfrontational to do this. Please examine the laws on your lens regarding communication. If the results you're creating in your marriage aren't meeting your needs, then there is probably an unsuitable law on your lens.

Let me suggest a simple and useful process to follow. Tell your spouse how it makes you feel when he or she does something you don't like. Ash him or her if that was his or her intention. If it was not, and he or she now knows how it made you feel, then you have a basis to ask him or her to stop doing it. And most times a spouse will. However, if your spouse's intention was to make you feel that way, then you have other issues to explore. But telling someone how you feel is the start of good communication.

This type of exchange works for Sherrie and me on most things.

- Ask your spouse if he or she knows how something makes you feel. "Do you know that when you make fun of my hair, it really hurts me?"
- Ask him or her if he or she wants you to feel that way. "Do you want me to feel hurt?"
- When he or she says no, tell him or her you assume they won't do it anymore.

It works. Try it.

Now let's look at some typical, everyday laws that might be on the lenses of married people. What about a law that says, "Cleaning is the wife's job"? What need might be driving a law like that? When that man's wife asks him to help vacuum, what is he likely to feel? Belittled, and maybe even angry. So what then is he likely to do? Refuse to help, maybe yell, maybe worse. Are the results going to meet his needs over time? No way.

What about the law on the lens, of either the husband or wife, that says, "The man is supposed to be the breadwinner"? Or a related law: "A mother should be at home with little children"? Ever know anybody with either of those laws? What need might be driving laws like that? What is the person with the first law going to feel if the husband loses his job? What will he or she feel if the wife has to go to work? The feelings probably won't be good, and the resulting behavior is not likely to be good either. It is, therefore, unlikely that the results will meet their needs over time.

We live in a time when divorce rates are extremely high. I wonder how many people go into their marriages today with a law on their lenses that says, "If things don't work out, I'll just get divorced"? With such a law, are they likely to spend any time working on problems? Is there any commitment to address problems together? When the going gets tough, these folks are gone in a heartbeat.

Unfortunately, we live in a society in which verbal and physical abuse are an everyday occurrence. I can't begin to even guess the laws that are on the lens of a man who physically abuses his wife. They say that many of these people were abused as children. The law must have been put on their lenses at a very early age, if they witnessed their father abusing their mother or were themselves abused. The even more puzzling phenomenon is the law on the lenses of some abused women that says, "I deserve it." Nobody deserves it. And if you think you have that law on your lens, you should seek help to either change your law or change your venue.

It is hard for me to understand why so many women stay in abusive relationships. I'm sure there are laws like, "I'm staying for the kids," or "It's my fault," or "He'll change," or "I have nowhere else to go." My answer is—take the kids with you, it isn't your fault, he won't change, and there is most definitely a place to go. But changing the laws on your lens takes courage. I don't mean to imply that it is easy. But it can be done.

There are thousands of laws on our lenses that pertain to marriage. How about these:

- Women should be submissive.
- My spouse should have sex with me whenever I want.
- Men take out the garbage and cut the grass.
- My wife better have dinner ready at 6 p.m. when I get home.

One of my favorites is the old fill-in-the-blank. This law says, "I'm _____ than my spouse." You can fill in the blank with any word you want—smarter, stronger, better looking, more talented, easier to get along with. The list goes on and on. Usually any law that defines you as different from other people, positively or negatively, will create results that will not meet your needs over time.

In closing this chapter, let me share one of the most common laws I see on the lenses of people getting married today. It says, "My spouse will change," or "I'll change him/her." And maybe you will, but what if you don't? Then where are you? First, I'm not sure anyone has the right to change another person. More importantly, what if you don't change him or her? If there is something that needs changing, please address it directly *before* you get married.

I'm not talking about simply changing a person's mind about something. I'm talking about changing a person's particular character trait. If your prospective spouse drinks too much now, he or she will drink too much after you're married. If he or she gambles, cheats, lies, beats you, he or she will do it after you're married. The best thing to do is to address any major character flaws before you get married. But after you're married, a much more healthy law would be, "I accept my spouse for who he or she is, and we'll work through any problems together."

8

Buddha, Muhammad, or Jesus— Take Your Pick

Rules of etiquette say you should never talk about religion or politics. I guess that's because most people have strong feelings, one way or another. My purpose in this chapter is not to say that anyone's laws are right or wrong, but rather to show that we all have laws about religion. They affect what we feel and do every day, and they constantly create results in our lives.

Let me just say up front that I am a Christian. I believe that Jesus Christ is my personal Lord and Savior. I acknowledge that many of the laws on my lens are based on this belief. But this chapter isn't about me, it is about how whatever religious laws are on your lens affect your life.

I would like to start with atheists and agnostics, or the absence of religion. For the sake of definition, an atheist denies the existence of God, whereas an agnostic claims no knowledge of God, but doesn't deny the possibility that God might exist. Statistics show that approximately 16 percent of the world's population, just over one billion people, fall into these categories. First, what need might be driving such a law? Maybe self-esteem or the need to feel important. But what does such a person feel when he or she sees a magnificent sunset or the birth of a child? I don't think non-believers see such things as miracles, but rather simply as events attributable to our natural environment.

As a result, they will feel something totally different from those who believe in God. Those feelings will influence what they do and the results they create. I'm sure that many atheists and agnostics would say that the results they're creating are meeting their needs over time. Those who believe in God might argue with them that results take time to measure, maybe even beyond death. I'm not saying the laws of atheists are wrong, just that that law will create different results from those who believe in God. And if at any point your results don't meet your needs, you should have the courage to change your laws.

The reason I personally struggle with the law that says, "There is no God," is because of design. If I told you that no one had designed my house, that one day the wind just blew and when it stopped, there stood my house, you'd think I was crazy. We would both know that wasn't true. The likelihood that the foundation, carpentry, masonry, plumbing, electricity, and painting all worked together so cohesively, without a designer or planner, is just incomprehensible.

When I look at the complexity of the human body and the intricacies of the nervous system, the cardiovascular and pulmonary system, the reproductive system, the digestive system, and so forth, I cannot help but conclude that there had to be a designer. I just don't believe that it all happened by chance.

So now we come to those who believe in God, or some form of Supreme Being. Just take a look at the following chart to see how many religions there are in the world.[5]

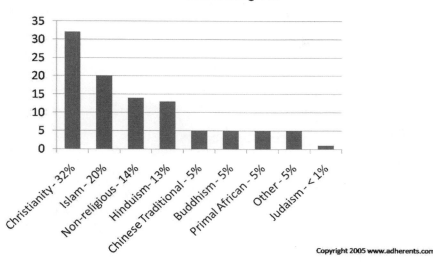

World Religions

Copyright 2005 www.adherents.com

In order by number of believers, these are the major religions:

- Christianity (2.1 billion)
- Islam (1.5 billion)
- Non-religious (atheists and agnostics) (1.1 billion)
- Hinduism (900 million)
- Chinese traditional (394 million)
- Buddhism (376 million)
- Primal-indigenous (African tribal) (300 million)
- Other (200 million)
- Judaism (14 million)

Briefly, let's examine the primary tenets of the major religions.

Christianity

Christianity is based a single triune of God the Father, Son, and Holy Spirit. God's Son Jesus came to earth as a man and died on a cross for the sins of the world. After three days he ascended into heaven and there reigns supreme.

The blanket term Christianity, as defined in the numbers above, includes every major denomination, including Catholic, Protestant, Orthodox, Pentecostal, Anglican, Mormon, Jehovah Witness, Quakers, and more. So even within Christianity, there is an enormously wide range of beliefs.

I'm not going to debate the differences in these denominations of Christianity. Each has its own unique beliefs. Catholics, for example, believe in purgatory, where most Protestants don't. Baptists believe that baptism should be full immersion, whereas other denominations either sprinkle water or pour water over the head of the person being baptized.

Most Christians, and most Jews as well, believe in the Ten Commandments as the accepted code of conduct for this life. One of the Ten Commandments says, "You shall not kill." Contrast that to Islam, for example, in which the Koran teaches that non-Muslims are infidels and should be killed. I'm not arguing that one is good or that one is bad. I'm arguing that they are almost direct opposites. As the world occurs for each of us, these laws create different feelings, different actions, and different results. With such contrasting laws on the lenses of the people of these faiths, is it any wonder we have war and terrorism?

Now I know that not all Muslims are terrorists, but if I ever met a hardcore Muslim terrorist who thought he needed to kill me because he considers me an infidel who doesn't believe in Allah, here is what I would say to him: "Would you rather have Allah, who tells you to kill me so that you can go to heaven; or would you rather have Jesus, who tells me to love you because *I am* going to heaven, and that He wants you to be with me?" Now that's a law change worth considering!

Since most readers of this book are likely to be Christians, I'd like to explore some of the more commonly held laws that can be found on the lenses of people of the Christian faith. How about a person with a law on his or her lens that says, "God couldn't possibly forgive me for what I've done"? When someone tells that person that forgiveness *is* possible, what will he or she feel? Probably disbelief, and then he or she will instantly reject such a notion.

What if that law could be replaced with another law that says, "Maybe God can forgive me"? Would that change anything? Of course, it could change everything! The person would be open to new possibilities, rather than rejecting those possibilities out of hand. What if that feeling led him or her to take action, to go to church, and to seek more wisdom about this new law? And what if somewhere down the road, he or she considered another law change, something like, "God has forgiven me"? Do you think a law change like that might make a difference in the results being created? Do you think that might better meet a person's needs over time? The possibilities are endless if you have the courage to examine your thoughts and then change the laws on your lens.

Below I've listed are few other religious laws that might be on the lens of Christians:

- God is keeping score, and if I don't hit the right number, then I won't get to heaven.
- Prayer doesn't change anything, so I don't bother anymore.
- The Bible can't be taken literally. There is no way Jonah lived in the belly of a whale for three days. Therefore, I'll pick and choose what I think is believable or fair.
- Confession doesn't cleanse *my* soul. I still feel as guilty as ever.
- Baptists are better than Catholics, so I'm not going to associate with Catholics.
- If you don't believe what I believe, then you're just wrong and I'm never going to let you forget it.
- All Muslims are terrorists and I'll never get on an airline with anybody wearing a turban.

Have you ever met another Christian who has laws like these? Me too. And this list could go on and on. Are your laws meeting your needs? If not, then *Please Change Your Mind.*

Lastly, I'd like to say that one of the hallmarks of Christianity is forgiveness. And forgiveness is nothing more than changing a law on your lens. Let's use an example to illustrate. Perhaps your wife has an affair, and in response you put a law on your lens that says, "My wife betrayed me and I will divorce her." This law is the truth. There is ample evidence to support it. Your wife did cheat on you. So if or when you decide to forgive her, you are changing that law. This is a powerful tool, and it's all in *your* hands.

I have read about people who forgive others who murdered their *families*. They changed their laws, and that will definitely change their results. God started it all when He forgave your sins.

Remember—if fear knocks and faith answers, no one is ever there!

Islam

Islam began in the seventh century and was established by Muhammad. Muslims follow the teachings of the Koran and strive to keep the five pillars—faith, prayer, giving, fasting, and pilgrimage.

Hinduism

The sacred writings of Hinduism date back to 1500 BC. Hindus have one supreme god—Brahma. Brahma has three separate forms—creator, preserver, and destroyer. But Hindus also have many other lesser gods, as many as 300 million of them.

I do not pretend to know any in-depth details of these religions, or the resulting laws that must exist on the lenses of all the people of these faiths. But I can tell you that those laws are different for each faith, and they produce unique and different results for each of them.

Buddhism

Buddhism was founded in approximately the sixth century BCE by Siddhartha Gautama. Buddhists believe that the ultimate goal in life is to be enlightened, as they perceive it. It has much in common with Hinduism in that both teach karma (cause-and-effect ethics), maya (the illusory nature of the world), and samsara (the cycle of reincarnation).

9

What Do I Do With These Kids?

It is my opinion that parenting is the most difficult job in the world. And the irony is that it is also the job for which you receive the least training. Suddenly one day you just are one. Nobody ever sat you down and told you the dos and don'ts of parenting. Stephen Covey didn't write a book called *The 7 Habits of Highly Effective Parents*. The only thing we really have to draw on is our perceptions of what our parents did that we considered right or wrong. Welcome to the toughest job in the world.

Just think, you created new life. And it is now your responsibility to prepare that child for anything and everything he or she is going to face in life. And you've got about eighteen years to do it. Daunting. Simply daunting.

The first year is a lot of sleep deprivation, diapers, and 2 a.m. feedings. After that, you begin to measure your child's growth by how much less stuff you have to carry around with you whenever you go out.

The first basic rule for good parenting is unconditional love. I know, because I grew up without it. I knew my parents loved me, but I always felt it was conditional. Love was predicated on performance or behavior, good grades, obedience, and following rules. I traded my entire childhood for *good boy*. When I was *good boy*, there was love, but when there was no *good boy*, there was no love. Make it a law on your lens that you will love your children unconditionally. More importantly, make sure they feel it. If you could ask my parents today if they loved me unconditionally, they would probably say yes. But because I never felt their love, it wasn't worth much to me.

One reason I was sure my father did not love me was his rule about not playing on Sundays. I was not allowed to play with my friends on Sundays. Sunday was a day of rest, of remembering the Sabbath and keeping it holy. That's a hard learning for a boy of ten. My friends made fun of me and ridiculed me. But the worst fallout of The Sunday Rule was in Little League. I was the star of my team, and all the other kids looked up to me. Each year the league had an All-Star game, and the All-Stars were elected by the players. I was elected every year. But because the All-Star game was always played on Sunday, I was never allowed to play. It was devastating. I cried in front of my teammates, who were genuinely sorry for me. I begged my father for a one-day exemption from The Sunday Rule, but he refused.

My conclusion at the time was that no father could love his child and still say no when his a son was begging to accept an honor bestowed on him by his peers. So the law I put on my lens was, "My dad doesn't love me." I know that he eventually came to realize that The Sunday Rule was bad, because he never enforced it with my younger brother, who was nine years younger than I. I had already moved out by that time. To my dad's credit, somewhere along the way he changed the law on his lens about no playing on Sunday. As an adult, I never had the courage to ask him about it, and he never had the courage to apologize to me.

There are two other laws that my parents placed on my lens, and to be honest, I probably still carry them both today. Oddly, they are opposites of each other. My most lasting memory of my mother is that she always told me that I could be anything I wanted, that I had no limitations. I could be president, an astronaut, an accountant, a fireman. It was all up to me. I believed her, and I still do. It is a law that will forever be on my lens, because the results meet my needs.

But from my father, my lasting memory is that I was a disappointment. I guess I heard him say, "I'm so disappointed in you," so many times that I came to believe I would always be a disappointment. In retrospect, I'm sure what he meant was that he was disappointed in what I had said or done at that particular moment. But what I heard was, "You're a disappointment." I've tried hard to shake that from my lens, but it's pretty stubborn. It's no wonder I was a rebellious teen. I was probably trying to hurt him as much as he had hurt me.

It would not be fair to my parents to leave you with the thought that they gave me only bad laws on my lens. They were fundamentally wonderful people with great values. They were family oriented, generous, kind, and thoughtful. My wife Sherrie will tell you that many of the positive laws on my lens came from my parents. Much of who I am today is because of them.

The point of all this is that as parents, you're putting laws on your kids' lenses every day without even knowing it. Make sure they hear, "I love you. It's what you *did* that I don't like."

Teens

The most dangerous thing that teens do is make decisions. So before your children get to be teens, it is essential that they have a lot of experience with decision making. The way you do that is to let them make plenty of decisions. You let three-year-olds make three-year-old decisions; that is, decisions that have little if any consequence, like what to wear. As they get older, you continue to let them make decisions commensurate with their age. The consequences get more significant, and your job is to explain the consequences to them, but the decision is theirs. You train them to analyze each decision and anticipate the consequences, positive or negative, before they decide. They will make mistakes; that's how they learn. Your job is to make sure that no decision is beyond their capability to assess the consequences, and that they don't try to make life-altering decisions.

So when they go off to college and really are on their own, they have years of training in decision making. If they've demonstrated that they are capable of making good decisions, you can then trust them to make good future decisions when on their own. The ability to make good decisions will definitely meet their needs over time.

The early years are also when you teach them the most about character traits. They learn this by watching you. Are you honest, generous, thoughtful, and loving? Are you a person of integrity, with high moral standards? Do you treat people with respect? Are you fair, and do you care about the feelings of others? They will see all this in your life, and they'll put laws on their lenses commensurate with what they observe in you. The character traits that you want for your children should also be specific topics of discussion, not just what they observe. Tell them the lifelong benefits of those traits you want to instill in them; tell them that they will meet their needs over time.

If you can get your family to believe in the *Please Change Your Mind* process, it will influence the language you use to approach conflict resolution. If your family starts talking about life in terms of laws, lenses, behaviors, results, and meeting needs, it will change the way you relate to one another. Strangers might think you are crazy, but it will work for you.

You can approach your teenage daughter about a particular behavior that you've observed in her, without seeming to be criticizing her. You can say things like, "Susie, I've noticed lately that you spend a lot of time alone in your room with your computer. I was just wondering if maybe you might have a new law on your lens. Can we discuss that?" This is not a personal attack on Susie. You're not talking about the Susie you love, you're not criticizing the Susie you love, you're just talking about a possible law on her lens. That is much more powerful.

And before you know it, your children will start asking you about laws they might see on your lens. Discuss those laws, and their subsequent feelings, behaviors, results, and needs at the dinner table. Ask your kids to talk about some of the laws they see in other kids, and what needs might be driving that law. All rather healthy stuff.

If you ever see a law on your child's lens that in any way suggests that their self-worth is based on externals, then you should seek to change that immediately. Their self-worth is not dependent on their clothes, their grades, the people they associate with, or the toys they have—whether that toy is a teddy bear or an iPad. They need to know that *they* determine their self-worth; that it is up to *them*, not anything external to them.

Before we close this chapter, let me give you a little list of some other parenting laws that you might see on parents' lenses. Take your time in reading them. See if they remind you of someone. Ask yourself whether they are potentially good or bad (by guessing whether the law will meet their needs over time). Ask yourself what need might be driving such a law.

- My kids better do what I say, or else.
- There are different rules for boys than there are for girls.
- Disciplining the kids is his/her job.
- All kids need discipline.
- All kids need to be spanked, at least occasionally.
- All kids need to be punished.
- I just want to be my kids' best friend.
- My kids' behavior is a direct reflection on me.
- Report cards are king. With a good report card, I'll let my kids do anything.
- It's okay to yell. I find it effective.
- I will control my kids' lives.
- My kids' performance in sports is a reflection on me, or my self-worth is dependent on how well my kids do in sports.
- My kids are _____ than yours (fill in the blank with any word—prettier, smarter, more athletic, etc.).

These are just a few examples. I'm sure you could name a hundred more. As parents, we all have laws on our lenses. Examine the ones that aren't meeting your needs and change them. Your kids will be the beneficiaries.

Good communication is essential to a healthy family. I know a cute story about family communication and family dynamics. One year, as all the other birds were flying south for the winter, one very young and brave bird decided to stay up north for another few weeks. Each day the weather got colder and colder, but the young bird was determined to stay up north until Thanksgiving. On that day, he finally headed south to join his family. But the faster and higher he flew, the colder he got. Suddenly it began to rain, and soon that rain turned to ice. The poor little bird struggled as hard as he could, but soon lost his strength and fell to the ground, landing in the middle of a barnyard.

He lay there exhausted and freezing to death. Just as he was about to give up, a cow came along and deposited her pie right on top of him. The warmth of the pie slowly melted the ice, and the little bird grew warmer. Soon he began feeling much better. He lifted his head up out of the pie and began chirping. The barnyard cat heard the chirping and came over to investigate the singing cow pie. The cat saw the bird's predicament and began digging the bird out of the cow pie. Once the bird was free, the cat ate it.

Now this story has three morals:

- Not everyone in the family who craps on you is your enemy.
- Not everyone in the family who takes crap off you is your friend.
- And when you're warm and comfortable, even if it's in a pile of crap, keep your mouth shut.

When my son was ten years old, he played Little League baseball. Out of that experience, I changed two major laws on my lens. The first change happened when, late in one game, the worst player on our team came up to bat. All the coaches and fans were shouting encouragement to him, me included. The kid swung and hit a ground ball between first and second base, but he did not sprint down to first base. In fact, he was going so slow, the right fielder threw the ball to first base and the kid was out. As he walked back to the dugout, though, he had a smile on his face. I remember yelling something like, "C'mon now, you have to hustle out there!" The man behind me in the stands put his hand on my shoulder and told me he had overheard my comment. He added, "That's my son. He has an artificial leg, and that was the first time he has ever hit the ball."

I could have crawled in a hole. I told the man how sorry I was, and suddenly I understood why the boy had had that smile on his face. I knew right then my law had to change. My new law says, "Never rush to judgment; you might not have all the facts." My results are now much better.

I changed the second law because of my own son. I was at his game, it was in the late innings, the score was tied, we had the bases loaded, and my son was coming up to bat. As I watched, I had an out-of-body experience. Suddenly I was observing the whole scene. I saw my son, the home team crowd cheering for him, the visiting team cheering against him, the coaches, and the umpires. And as I looked at my son, I wondered what must be going through his mind. As I thought about it from his perspective, I realized the pressure he must be under.

I decided right then to change my law from "Little League baseball is important" to "Little League baseball is just supposed to be fun for kids." I was so struck by that moment that I wrote a poem about it. I'd like to share it with you.[5]

TEN

The stands are filled with parents,
There is tension in the air.
The fielders are in position,
As the pitcher assumes his stare.
The bases are all loaded,
It is his team's last at bat;
Two are out, one run behind,
He stands and removes his hat.
He walks to the on-deck circle,
Filled with a thousand fears,
Selects his bat, and takes his stance,
As the crowd noise fills his ears.
His dad yells, "You can do it,
We're depending on you, son."
Mom says, "Get a hit now,
And drive in those two runs."
The other stands yell also,
"He's a bum, this guy can't hit."
The pitcher starts his wind-up,
As the catcher bangs his mitt.
The batter swings and misses,
The umpire screams, "Strike one."
His coach now apprehensive, says,
"Be a hitter in there, son."
The pitcher winds again,
The spectators' eyes like glue
On the man behind the plate,
Who screams again, "Strike two."
"I told you this guy's a bum,"
Comes thundering from the stands,
"It only takes one," Dad says
As he stoops to dry his hands.

His teammates shout support,
He cannot let them down,
All eyes on the pitcher now
As he glares out toward the mound.
The crowd begins to quiet
As the pitcher starts to throw,
The home stands sigh relief,
As the umpire says, "Ball, low."
The pressure mounts for everyone,
Both crowds stand and scream,
"We're depending on you, son," and
"He's a bum and so's his team!"
In quiet anticipation,
With the count now three and two,
All eyes are focused on the plate,
What will the batter do?
The boy looks up at the umpire
And asks that time be called,
The coaches in amazement
And both crowds seem appalled.
The batter looks at everyone,
Droops his head, and then
Lonely, confused, and scared, thinks,
"Don't they know I'm only ten?"

In case you're wondering what my son really did at the end of that game—
I'll never tell. That's the whole point, it doesn't matter. What matters is
that I hugged him afterward and we went for ice cream.

10

But I Hate Dieting and Workouts

With the recent Affordable Care Act, the subject of health care in general has been in the forefront of the minds of most Americans. The whole objective of health care from an individual's perspective is to be and stay healthy. So let's understand what the experts have to say about getting healthy and staying healthy.

Approximately 2.4 million people died in the United States in 2007.[6] The causes of death are shown in the table below:[7]

Cause of Death	Number of Deaths	Percentage of Total
Heart Disease	631,636	26.3%
Cancer	599,888	24.9%
Stroke	137,119	5.7%
Respiratory Disease	124,583	5.2%
Accidents	121,599	5.1%
Diabetes	72,449	3.0%
Alzheimer's Disease	72,432	3.0%
Flu & Pneumonia	56,326	2.3%
Kidney Disease	45,344	2.0%
Septicemia (blood poison)	34,234	1.5%
All Other	504,390	21.0%
TOTAL	2,400,000	100.0%

As you can see, 51.2 percent of the deaths in the United States in 2007 were from heart disease and cancer. Doctors and researchers tell us that the best way to avoid heart disease is to maintain a normal weight, eat a healthy diet, and exercise regularly. This is not rocket science. The experts have been telling us this for years. Do you know why? Because it works!

Diet

America is fat. And getting fatter. After all the health warnings, doctor recommendations, and FDA regulations, plus a massive weight-loss industry, Americans are packing on the pounds at an alarming rate. In the past year, obesity rates for adults in thirty-three states were over 25 percent.[8] In those states, one in four people is considered obese. So who is to blame? Is it the fattening ingredients in our diet, predatory marketing, overeating, not enough exercise, or is it just a simple lack of self-control? The reality is that it is all of these.

The generally accepted definition of obesity is more than 20 percent over your ideal weight. So for a woman whose ideal weight is 135, anything over 162 would be considered obese. For a man whose ideal weight is 200, anything over 240 would be considered obese. But morbidly obese is anybody who is more than 100 pounds over his or her ideal weight.

According to the US Centers for Disease Control and Prevention, in 2008, 34 percent of adults over age twenty were obese.[9] Another 34 percent were considered overweight. A third of overweight people, 55 percent of obese people, and 59 percent of morbidly obese people say they eat too much of the wrong types of food. Add to that the 60 percent of Americans who say they don't exercise as much as they should.

So with all these statistics, how many people do you know with a law on their lenses that says, "I'll lose weight next year," or "I'm not *that* overweight"? Or even worse, "Yeah, I'm a little overweight, but my health is good," or "I really don't watch what I eat very much"? What need might be driving laws like that? I'm not sure. But I know what those people will feel when they're offered pizza, or doughnuts, or dessert. They'll feel justified. And what will they do? You bet that they'll eat that stuff without batting an eye, even when they might be morbidly obese.

I have struggled with my weight all my life. I have weighed as much as 300 pounds. In the course of my life, I have probably gained and lost the equivalent weight of six or seven people. As I have examined my lens for the laws that exist when I'm heavy, and they say things like, "Eat what you want, it's okay." But sixty to a hundred pounds later, you realize that it isn't okay and you start another diet. The laws on my lens during those successful dieting periods are things like, "I'm not healthy. To get healthy I must watch my food intake and really eat more healthy foods." In order for me to have sustained success with my weight, I need a law that says, "This is not a diet, this is how you need to eat for the rest of your life." I'm working hard on that now.

Recently a good friend of my wife lost her father. When he died he weighed over 400 pounds and could not even get out bed. He was finally taken to a nursing home, where he died. My wife's friend confirmed that her father always believed he could eat whatever he wanted, whenever he wanted. That law certainly didn't meet his needs over time.

Regular Checkups

Be honest. Do you even remember the last time you went to a doctor for a complete physical? A routine physical can detect problems early on while treatment is still an option, or while a diagnosis can be easily made. Putting off a physical can lead to serious complications, because many illnesses and diseases have no early physical symptoms. If caught soon enough, many problems can be treated with high degrees of success. Prostate cancer in men and breast cancer in women are treated much more successfully when detected early.

Mammograms, pap smears, colonoscopies, PSA tests, and blood chemistry analysis should be a regular part of your health care process. I've read recently that annual physicals should be done twice in your twenties, three times in your thirties, four times in your forties, and then every year thereafter. Going more often sure won't hurt you.

But how many people do you know who have a law that says, "I feel great, I don't need a physical," or "When I feel bad, then I'll go to the doctor." Some people are in denial and have a law that says, "Yeah, my cholesterol is high, but it'll be okay." Are laws like those going to meet their needs over time? Are they going to create the results they want in their lives? Probably not. If you won't change your laws about regular checkups for yourself, please do it for your family. They want you around for a long time.

The first annual physical I ever had was alarming. None of my blood chemistry was good. My cholesterol was high, my uric acid was high, my triglycerides were high, my blood pressure was high, my heart rate was high, I was overweight, I smoked, and there was blood in my urine. My doctor really scared me—as he should have.

What made it worse was my heredity. My mother had very high cholesterol and high blood pressure. She smoked a pack of unfiltered cigarettes every day of her adult life, and quite predictably she died at the age of sixty-six. Given her history, I took my doctor's advice to heart. I went on several medications immediately. Then I started dieting, quit smoking, and started running. My laws went from "Eat whatever you want, exercise sucks, and I really enjoy cigarettes," to "My life needs transformation."

Within six months, I lost sixty pounds, quit smoking, and ran a marathon. Now that's transformation. For some reason I really fell in love with running, and when you're running fifty miles a week, you really can eat whatever you want. But when you stop running, which years later I eventually did, I needed to change my eating laws, but I didn't. Predictably, I gained weight. This is proof that you constantly need to be examining the laws on your lens and making changes where and when they are appropriate.

Exercise

This goes hand in hand with wanting to lose weight. But trends show that sedentary habits are hard to overcome. In a 2008 Gallup poll, Americans were asked how frequently they participate in:

- Moderate sports or recreational activities
- Vigorous sports or recreational activities
- Weight lifting or weight training

The percentage of people reporting regular participation (three times per week) has shown virtually no movement since 2001. The data suggest that only half of Americans meet the requirements for getting enough exercise.

Experts say that moderate exercise (for example, walking at a pace that elevates your heart rate and causes you to sweat a little) five days per week for just thirty minutes is sufficient. Vigorous exercise is better, and when combined with some weight training, it is the best. There are obvious variances for age and health, but it is easily done by most everyone.

I learned the lesson of exercising regularly again in 2010. After all the years of running for myself and in marathons, I was back up to nearly 300 pounds. As a New Year's resolution (which is nothing more than changing a law on your lens, by the way), I hired a personal trainer. She created a regimen for me that involved core exercises, upper and lower body strength exercises, and aerobics. At the same time I was eating less food, and more healthy food.

By August I had lost sixty-five pounds, and I won an award at my club, which my trainer deserved as much as I did. It is more than willpower and self-control. Because I changed the law on my lens, the whole world occurred differently for me. Food came through my lens as something good, but to be controlled. Exercise came through my lens as enjoyable, something that was creating the results I wanted, and boy, was it ever meeting my needs. It wasn't a daily battle. When my law changed, it became something I wanted to do.

Do you know any people with a law on their lenses that says, "I don't have time to work out," or "I'm not overweight, I don't need to work out," or "Working out is so boring, working out is too much like work, I don't like to sweat or get out of breath?" We've heard all these laws and many more. But it probably won't meet those people's needs over time. As you get older, it is harder to lose weight because your metabolism slows down. You'll need all that muscle mass to burn calories and build bone density. For most of us, Mother Nature and the aging process catches us by surprise.

Smoking

It is estimated that there are 47 million smokers in the United States today, 23 percent of adults and 30 percent of adolescents.[10] Nearly a quarter million people will be diagnosed with lung cancer this year. Lung cancer is the second most common cancer and the leading cause of cancer deaths for both men and women.

The FDA has long required warnings on cigarette packages that essentially say, "These things will kill you, stupid!" Yet so many people continue to smoke. The FDA has now proposed a new rule for warnings on cigarette packages, which includes nine textual warnings. They are listed below:

- Cigarettes are addictive.
- Tobacco smoke can harm your children.
- Cigarettes cause fatal lung disease.
- Cigarettes cause cancer.
- Cigarettes cause heart disease and strokes.
- Smoking during pregnancy can harm your baby.
- Smoking can kill you. *(How plain can they be?)*
- Tobacco smoke causes fatal lung disease in nonsmokers.
- Quitting smoking now greatly reduces serious risk to your health.

Even secondhand smoke is extremely dangerous. And smokers don't have to fear just lung cancer. Emphysema can kill you too. I had an uncle who died of emphysema. You basically lose lung capacity over time, until ultimately you suffocate. It was terrible to watch him suffer. And while he had quit smoking years before, the damage had been done.

My mother was a smoker until the day she died. And while she didn't get lung cancer or emphysema, she died at a comparatively young age. It was a predictable death. She smoked a pack a day, her cholesterol level was over three hundred, she never exercised, and she put butter in the pan before she fried bacon. One morning after she had her coffee, she went back to bed with a headache and never woke up. She died of a cerebral hemorrhage.

The whole family had scolded her many times that she was killing herself. Even worse, she was making us watch her commit suicide. She had a law on her lens that said, "It won't hurt me." And right up until the day she died, that law met her needs. She felt good, had plenty of energy, and had no outward signs of any disease. But in the end, her law did not meet her needs. The results she created for herself were not visible. She couldn't see the manifestation of her lifestyle under her skin.

My poor father, who adored her, had to live another twenty years without her, and her laws certainly didn't meet his needs either. If you smoke, ask yourself what need might be driving that behavior. Examine the law(s) on your lens that might be justifying or rationalizing your habit. It might seem to be meeting your needs right now, but results take time to measure. It took my mother sixty-six years to realize that her needs really were not being met. Don't wait that long.

Let me tell you about my experience when I quit smoking. Perhaps it will help you, as well as make clearer for you the power of changing laws on your lens. Quitting smoking was easy for me. Here's why. I started by acknowledging that it is never hard to do what you want to do. Nobody has trouble doing what they want to do. When I quit smoking, I wanted to be a nonsmoker more than I wanted to smoke. My new law said that. When I wanted to be thin more than I wanted to eat, I never had trouble dieting. My new law said that. Weight Watcher's has a saying: "Nothing tastes as good as thin feels." If the law on your lens is something you really want to do, it will never be hard to do.

Disease

Probably the three scariest diseases for Americans are HIV, AIDS, and STDs (sexually transmitted diseases). STDs can be painful, irritating, debilitating, and even fatal. More than twenty STDs have been identified.

They occur most commonly in sexually active teenagers and young adults, especially those with multiple sex partners. According to the US Department of Health and Human Services, more than thirteen million Americans are infected each year, and more than sixty-five million worldwide have an incurable STD.[11] Generally, STD incidence has declined over the last fifteen years, although rates in certain classes, like gay men, have increased. It is estimated that two hundred to four hundred million people worldwide are infected with an STD—representing men and women of all economic classes.

In 2009, it was estimated that the number of people living with HIV/AIDS worldwide exceeded thirty-three million.[12] Just over half of these were women. The number of people with HIV rose from about eight million in 1990 to the thirty-three million at the end of 2009, a 400 percent increase in twenty years.

The annual number of new HIV infections has steadily declined in recent years, due to the significant increase in people receiving antiretroviral therapy. Over 68 percent of the people living with the AIDS virus live in Africa, another 12 percent live in Southeast Asia, and just over 4 percent in the United States. Since the beginning of the epidemic in the early 1980s, nearly thirty million people have died from AIDS-related causes.

In the United States, an estimated 1.5 million people are living with HIV, and nearly one million have died after developing AIDS. In 2009, there were an estimated 50,000 new diagnoses of HIV infection. Over 75 percent of those infected are men. There are approximately 18,000 AIDS-related deaths in the United States each year, and the estimated total deaths since the epidemic began is 750,000.[13]

My former sister-in-law had a gay brother. He had a partner and they lived together. I have no idea if they were exclusive or had many different sexual partners. Eventually we learned that he had contracted AIDS. He died the next year, only in his twenties. Later his partner died, and my guess is that he was in his thirties. I confess that I did not know either one very well. I do know that it was horrible for their families to go through that experience. It is not a natural thing for parents to bury their children. I cannot possibly begin to know the laws that existed on the lenses of those two young men. And I do not know the needs they had that drove those laws. But I do know that those laws didn't meet their needs over time.

So with all these statistics, how is it possible that so many young men have laws on their lenses that say, "I don't need to wear a condom, I won't catch anything," or "I only have sex with girls I know, so I know they're clean," or "I assume the needle is clean when I shoot up." Are you kidding me? C'mon guys, get with the program. This is serious stuff. And you girls need to make sure you're just as careful when protecting yourselves. The laws listed above will *not* meet your needs over time.

The Ordeal

I had a law on my lens for a long time that said, "Sherrie and I will grow old together." I don't take that law for granted anymore. Two years ago Sherrie asked me if her skin looked yellow. It didn't look yellow to me. But the next day it was obvious that she was jaundiced. She made an appointment with our regular doctor, and he ran some blood tests because he thought it might be hepatitis. The results of the blood tests were negative, so our doctor referred us to a gastroenterologist. That doctor said there probably was some blockage in the common bile duct that was backing up into the liver and causing the jaundice. Typically, this can be a gall stone. He needed to go in with a scope, find the blockage, and remove it.

When he went in with the scope, he found nothing inside the bile duct that could cause a blockage, so he put in a stent to allow things to flow normally from the liver to the pancreas. The bad news was, if there was no blockage on the inside like a gall stone, then something had to be pushing on the bile duct from the outside, stopping normal flow. It was like a garden hose that wouldn't spray water. If nothing was inside the hose blocking normal flow, then someone must be standing on the hose, right?

We asked the doctor what could be pushing on the bile duct. The answer wasn't good. He said that most likely it was some type of mass or tumor, and that he needed to go back in to see. We scheduled another scope procedure. This time, the camera would not be inside the bile duct but outside it, looking for a cause. We knew a little about the pancreas. A couple of years earlier a friend ours, a pathologist, had lost her father to pancreatic cancer. We knew that a mass on the pancreas was malignant 98 percent of the time.

No one really survives pancreatic cancer; it is just a matter of how much time you have. Therefore, any diagnosis of pancreatic cancer is a death sentence. We scheduled the scope and prayed for a good result. The day of the procedure, Sherrie and I were both extremely nervous and obviously scared. I was waiting anxiously in the waiting room, when the doctor came in to give me the results.

First he told me that Sherrie was in the recovery room and doing fine, and then he said the procedure had gone fine. I didn't care about any of that. I wanted to know what he had found, so I interrupted him and asked, "Did you find a mass?" He paused, like he was trying to avoid giving me any bad news. Then he said, "I'm afraid we did. I took a biopsy and sent it to pathology for testing." After that, I didn't hear another word he said.

I went into the recovery room and found Sherrie. I thought she would still be groggy from the anesthesia, but she was awake and asked me straightaway if they had found a mass. I completely lost it. I leaned down and hugged her and told her that they had found a mass a little bigger than a golf ball. We cried. The nurses cried. It was the worst moment of my life. It's not every day that you have to tell your wife that she is going to die.

All this happened on a Wednesday. We would get the pathology report on Friday, and we were clinging to that 2 percent chance. Friday came, and we learned that the biopsy was not viable. There was not enough tissue to test. We wanted to get another biopsy as soon as possible, but the soonest we could do that was Monday. But the following Monday was a holiday. We had to wait until Tuesday.

That was the longest weekend of our lives. The next Tuesday we went back for the second biopsy. This time the doctors went through Sherrie's back and got a viable sample. Now all we could do was wait again. Meanwhile we had been talking to our pathologist friend, who at our request was now involved with the pathologists at the hospital. We learned from her that there was a new operation called a Whipple, which had shown promising results. But it was considered a serious and dangerous surgery.

About this time I succumbed to the 98 percent mentality. I changed the law on my lens to: "I don't have Sherrie for much longer. Make the most of every minute." We were supposed to get the results on Wednesday, and we waited at home for the news. Sherrie's sister, our daughter, and our two-year-old twin grandsons were with us. The call came about one o'clock from our pathologist friend, who had gone to the hospital to see the results. I answered the phone, and she told me it was benign! I started crying. Enormous tears ran down my face. Everybody else thought it was bad news because of my tears, but they were tears of joy. As soon as I hung up, I shouted, "It's benign!" We had a long group hug, and everybody was crying. So in the course of one week, I had told my wife that she was going to die, and then I got to tell her that I was only kidding. Talk about an emotional roller coaster.

I have no idea how large the prayer network was for Sherrie. It was in the thousands, I know. Sherrie doesn't believe for one minute that she was in the lucky 2 percent. She believes with all her heart that she was in the 98 percent and that God chose to heal her, in no small part due to all the fervent prayers. We agreed that she still had something important to do in her life.

The gastroenterologist had done his homework. Sherrie's condition was called autoimmune pancreatitis. He learned that doctors in Japan had treated this condition successfully with massive doses of steroids. So she started the treatment. In ninety days she had another scan to see what impact the steroids had had on the mass. The results were not good. They were great! The mass was completely gone. Not shrunk, but *gone!* Can that be explained in any way other than God did it? You'll never convince me. You'll never convince Sherrie. It is the only explanation in our book.

So I've changed my law again, and now it says, "I'm going to grow old with Sherrie, but I'll never take a single day with her for granted." I'm likin' the results and it's meetin' my needs, baby!

11

Hey, Hey, Hey—Let's Be Careful Out There

All of us have laws on our lenses about safety. The obvious need that is driving these safety laws is to be safe and to live. You probably have many positive laws in this regard, such as:

- Don't touch fire.
- Don't jump off high places.
- Don't play in the street.

When you're in situations that threaten these laws, you generally feel afraid and you avoid them. You don't touch fire, you don't jump off the roof, and you don't play in the street. This creates results in your life that you like. Therefore, they are proven to meet your needs over time.

But you also might have some safety laws that don't meet your needs over time. What about when you need to make a quick trip to the store? Do you have a law that says, "I don't need to lock the house, I'll be right back"? I'm not saying this is a bad law. It may be working fine for you so far, and it may work for you the rest of your life. But I know people who have left their houses unlocked, using that same reasoning, and their results ended up not meeting their needs.

I grew up riding in cars that had no seat belts. You can't wear them if they're not there, right? As a consequence, I put the law on my lens, at a very young age, that it was okay to drive without a seat belt on. Today, my grandkids have never been in a car that doesn't have seat belts, and they have never ridden without their seat belts on. The law on their lenses is that you always wear your seat belt. Over time I have changed my law, because I can see that the possible results might not meet my needs over time.

I see people out there all the time riding without their seat belts on, and that might be meeting their needs for now. They apparently just don't consider that results take time to measure, and that their positive results could change in a second. Some teenagers who drive seem to have a law on their lenses that says, "I'm invincible, I'm indestructible, and I will live forever." Do you think a person with a law like that is going to a wear seat belt? Or use a condom? Or stop smoking?

If you really want to change that teenager, you don't focus on the behavior. It's not about the seat belts, or the condoms, or the cigarettes. It's all about that lousy law on his lens. If you can change that law, all the behaviors take care of themselves.

When I was growing up, not only did I not wear a seat belt, I never wore a helmet when I rode my bike. Of course, there were no bike helmets when I was a kid. I had a paper route, delivering papers in my neighborhood, and I did that until I was fourteen years old. I never had an accident. So naturally, the law that I didn't need to wear a helmet worked for me. When I was in my early twenties, though, I was riding a friend's motorcycle. I was just going to take it around block. It was wintertime, and the town had sanded the roads because of the snow.

But the snow had melted, so there was sand on the dry pavement. I took a turn a little too fast, laid the bike down, and both the bike and I slid under a parked car. I spent a week in the hospital with head injuries. When

I left the hospital, I had a new law on my lens about the value of helmets. In fact, my new law says, "Never ride motorcycles," and I haven't been on another one since.

When I was a kid, we never had smoke detectors or alarms in our house. There was no such thing as a smoke alarm. You can't have them if they don't exist. But everyone knows that the danger of a house fire is very real. Today, the value of smoke alarms is virtually unchallenged. They are so valuable, in fact, that the insurance industry has a law on its lens that says, "If you don't have smoke detectors in your home, we will charge higher rates." Some safety laws are so important that if you don't put that law on your lens, somebody else will do it for you.

I pay over two hundred dollars each year for a security alarm system for my home. If a door or window is breached, the worst noise you've ever heard in your life starts blaring in your ears. We even have motion detectors, which my cat loves to set off. At the beginning of 2010, I told my wife that I wanted to cancel our home security system. Here was my reason—nobody was going to break into our house. It hadn't happened for ten years, and it was so unlikely to happen that we just didn't need to take that precaution and incur that expense anymore. Sherrie argued with me. And she was right. While my law was meeting my needs, results take time to measure. And just because we'd had no break-in for the past ten years, didn't mean that we might not have one tomorrow. She effectively changed my law. And just for the record, when I was a kid, there was no such thing as a home security system either!

I have four-year-old twin grandsons. With little ones around, you become sensitive to keeping certain things out of reach—things like knives on countertops, hot cups of coffee, and other household items that can be dangerous. But four-year-olds have no clue. When they get a little older, you tell them not to touch certain things. After you have told them these rules a hundred times, it is easy to develop a law that says, "My kids won't touch that." And if you're lucky, they won't.

But I have a friend who was cooking fried chicken in an electric frying pan on her countertop. Her daughter Kim was toddling around and grabbed the power cord. The hot grease spilled onto Kim's head, down the side of her face, onto her arm, and down her leg. She was rushed to the hospital, and the family spent years in the recovery and rehab process. Of course, the mother blamed herself. Needless to say, her law quickly changed to, "If my kids can reach it, they *will* touch it." I am happy to say that today that little girl has graduated from college and has only a small scar on the side of her face.

We all have laws on our lenses about all kinds of safety—home safety, driving safety, child safety, and personal safety. We take precautions every day commensurate with the laws on our lenses. But with any safety law, just because it hasn't happened so far doesn't mean it won't happen tomorrow. The insurance industry exists because we want to mitigate our risk. Just remember that results take time to measure.

12

Hold It Right There, Louie, and Drop That Gun

It may seem strange to have a chapter about law enforcement in a book like this, but I think it is extremely appropriate. Who would have more laws on their lenses than officers of the law?

Our police officers have one of the most difficult jobs in America. They have to enforce the law, keep the peace, and not anger anyone, all without getting hurt. A pretty impossible task.

Most everybody remembers the Rodney King incident in Southern California, in which several police officers were accused of abusing a suspect. The incident was caught on tape, with multiple officers hitting Rodney King with their batons. When a jury found the officers innocent, it sparked a riot. Needless to say, that created a nightmare for the Los Angeles police commissioner and the entire police force. My guess is that some of those officers had a law on their lenses that went something like this: "When a suspect resists arrest, I have the right to beat him or her until he or she does what I say." Perhaps their law says, "When a suspect endangers innocent people, it just infuriates me; and when I catch them, my first thought is to beat them." Or maybe it says, "When my life is in danger, I'm justified to use any force necessary." I'm not saying that any of these laws are bad. It is very understandable to me how such laws get placed on the lenses of police officers.

There is a wonderful book written by Dr. George Thompson entitled *Verbal Judo*. The book was written with law enforcement officers in mind. However, it is applicable to anyone who works with the public—customer service agents, bank tellers, salespeople, flight attendants, and so on. The purpose of the book is to teach people to get the results they want from others by using words—what the book calls voluntary compliance. It is all about contact professionalism.

For police officers, it is getting others to do what they want with words; for customer service agents, it is conflict resolution with words; for families, it is achieving harmony with words; and for businesses, it is achieving goals and building consensus with words.

The book teaches, for example, that when a suspect calls a policeman a pig, he or she can ignore that, as long as the suspect is doing what he or she wants. If the suspect is not resisting arrest, then let him or her say whatever he or she wants. The book teaches officers not to *react* to situations, but rather to *respond* to them; not to rush to judgment; and always to stay in control of their actions.

Verbal Judo teaches officers to show respect and to consider the viewpoint of the other person at all times. It suggests that all of us should give others a way to save face. It is about listening first and talking second. And it tells readers that when they lose their temper, they also lose their common sense.

It is no wonder that so many law enforcement agencies use *Verbal Judo* as part of their ongoing training. It is excellent, and I highly recommend it. But the essence of the book suggests powerful new laws that readers should put on their lenses.

If all you do is focus on your behavior or someone else's behavior, you will only get short-term results. Behavior is never the problem; it is simply the symptom of the problem. The problem is the law on the person's lens that is dictating his or her behavior. If you are a bigoted white Southern police officer and you have a law on your lens that says, "White people are better than black people," what are you likely to do when you come across a white boy fighting with a black boy? You're probably going to arrest the black boy and let the white boy go.

If your sergeant tells you that your behavior was unacceptable and that you need to change it, you will probably make some effort to do so. And you might really do better for a while. But with that law still on your lens, it is only a matter of time before you lapse into other unacceptable behavior. And maybe this time the result is a charge of police brutality, which will not meet your needs or those of your commissioner. Making a positive change in your life is not about changing your behavior; it is about changing your mind. It is about changing that law on your lens.

Let me share a few of the laws that you might find on the lens of a law enforcement officer, and then place next to it a different law that could replace it. As you look at these contrasting laws, consider the needs that might be driving them, what the officer might be feeling and how he or she might then behave, the likely results of his or her behavior, and whether or not those results will meet his or her needs over time. Do this for both sets of laws:

- "Some people just don't deserve respect" versus "I should respect everyone."
- "If a suspect doesn't do what I say, I'll give him or her a thump with my baton" versus "I only use force as a last resort."
- "All Hispanics are here illegally" versus "All people are here legally until proven otherwise."
- "I carry a gun and I'll use it" versus "I carry a gun and hope I never have to use it."
- "Customers are such a pain" versus "The customer is always right."
- "I don't have to be courteous anymore after someone has been rude" versus "I am always courteous."
- "It's okay to lose my temper with my kids when they're wrong" versus "I will always maintain my self-control."
- "I'll never sell the business to Bob" versus "I should listen to all legitimate offers."

You can make up as many of these contrasting laws as you want. The behavior in each one is predictable and so are the results. But don't focus on changing the behavior. As I said, the behavior is only the symptom of the problem. You must change your *mind* and get rid of that law on your lens that isn't working for you anymore.

I have an uncle who is retired from the Baltimore Police Department. I also have a friend who is currently on the police force in the county where I grew up. I have ridden with him all night on the graveyard shift and observed police life up close and personal. These men and women leave their homes every day, kissing their spouses good-bye but with no more idea if they'll be home for dinner than the man in the moon.

They risk their lives every time they get in their squad cars. They deserve our admiration and respect.

Customer Service

There are many vocations that require people to deal with the public—flight attendants, ticket agents, bank tellers, and even cab drivers. They all have laws on their lenses about how to deal with the public in a variety of situations. I have a friend who works for a bank, with nearly one hundred branches under her management. The bank provides extensive training for their employees to help them better deal with customers. In this training, the bank in essence is trying to put laws on its employees' lenses so they can provide the best service possible.

Interestingly, the bank thinks it has done too good a job. In its zeal to promote "good service" laws on the employees' lenses, the bank is finding that employees don't always listen long enough to a customer's problem. Instead, they jump immediately to a solution, trying to resolve the situation, only to find out that they didn't listen long enough to understand the full problem. Their suggested solution was both premature and insufficient. As a result, the training has changed to create a law that says, "Listen to the customer and ask questions, until you are sure you fully understand the problem you are trying to resolve."

13

The Only Unit That Matters

I grew up in what I would call a normal family of the 1950s and early 1960s. My family consisted of Mom and Dad and one younger brother. Most all my friends were in a similar family structure. Very few, if any, lived in a divorce situation, with only one parent at home.

Not one girl in my high school graduating class of 1965 had to leave school because she got pregnant. Nobody I knew was doing drugs of any kind. We drank beer and smoked cigarettes, and a few were having sex on a regular basis, but that was the extent of our wild activities.

Today, almost all kids are exposed to different kinds of drugs, alcohol, and sex. The worst thing that could happen to me was to get caught with a beer and a cigarette and get punished.

Today, kids have much more to lose than I did. Sex for me might have meant a pregnancy; sex today might mean an STD or HIV. Beer for me was a parental restriction; alcohol and drugs today can mean a police record. Kids today face life-altering consequences for their actions that I never faced. Children today can hear and see things on television that I couldn't even see in the movies in 1965. Kids today are exposed to things that I wasn't exposed to until I was in my mid-twenties.

Our culture today is completely different. When I was growing up, I went to church every Sunday; most kids today don't. In my time, most kids had two parents at home; today, maybe only 75 percent have two parents at home. In my time, there was no welfare or food stamps; today, over thirty million people are on welfare. In my day, births to single mothers was only 6 percent. Today it is 40 percent.[14]

Here are some more alarming statistics:[15]

- Forty percent of all youth today are born out of wedlock; for minorities, the figure is 72 percent.
- Sixty-three percent of youth suicides are from fatherless homes.
- Ninety percent of all homeless and runaway children come from a fatherless home.
- Eighty percent of rapists come from a fatherless home.
- Seventy-one percent of high-school dropouts come from a fatherless home.
- Eighty-five percent of all youths in prison today grew up in a fatherless home.
- Thirty-three percent of *all* children in America today do not live with their fathers. For African Americans, the figure is 64 percent.

What's happened to us? What about those wedding vows? What happened to all the dads? I believe that all this culture change originates with the breakdown of the family unit. And I think it all started with the advent of Social Security, when the government decided it needed to take care of us.

For some reason, the government has decided that it can take care of us better than we can take care of ourselves. It feels it needs to, and we let it. Little by little, we have abdicated family responsibilities to other places. We changed the law on our lenses that said, "I can and should take care of myself," to "Well, if the government wants to do it, I'll let it." And that law has changed yet again, so that it seems to say, "I'm entitled to have the government take care of me!"

Families are important, yet they always seem to be sacrificed for other things that are urgent. George Barna said in his book *The Future of the American Family*, "Most Americans do not have a philosophy of life. This missing component renders them powerless to overcome the tyranny of the urgent. Decisions are made without an understanding of what is and is not important; we often fail to see what are the best means of accomplishing the goals in our life (if we have even identified such goals). Until we can create a mental map of what is important to us, the chances that we will arrive at a fulfilling destination are minimal."[16]

I submit to you that the law on the lenses of too many Americans is this: "Family is not as important as the urgent things I need to do."

Even in homes today that have both a mother and father, their schedules are so hectic that they rarely eat dinner together. If both parents work, it is hard.

Between work, driving kids to baseball, gymnastics, Boy Scouts and Girl Scouts, ballet, and karate, there just isn't a lot of time left to cook dinner and have everyone sit down to eat together. When did we get so busy? When did we change the law on our lenses to say, "Our kids should be involved in everything"? Have we subtly exchanged one law for another—a law of spending time together as a family, for a law of independence and trying to experience everything that comes along?

The courts haven't helped. Court rulings and interpretations on both free speech and legal abortion are probably not what our forefathers intended. In addition, the American Civil Liberties Union (ACLU) has played a role in the rulings of the judicial branch. And of course the Internet has just made access to everything easier.

But we as a people have abdicated family responsibility to others. Remember when sex education was taught at home and not at school? How about the English language? In 1965, I didn't know one immigrant who didn't speak English. Remember when there was a dress code? Remember when we taught table manners at home? Remember when Grandpa got too old to live alone and he came to live with you? I remember those days. What happened to us? We've lost our sense of family.

Families are important because they are our past, they are our blood, they want the best for us, they teach us about life, and they love us unconditionally. If we can get *that* back, we can get our *country* back.

Let me tell you a little about my family. My mom was a caregiver. You didn't even have to be family. If you needed help, she was there. My dad believed family came before all else. When I was a little kid, we went to visit grandparents, aunts, uncles, and cousins all the time.

If you were family, my dad would move heaven and earth for you. We had dinner together every night. And every night after dinner, weather permitting, my dad played catch with me in the front yard, no matter how tired he was. My parents taught me morals, ethics, courtesy, respect for others, honesty, courage, thoughtfulness, and on and on. When I think back on it now, I realize that they taught me things that today I just take for granted. I absorbed their example and their values into my core essence by osmosis.

My aunt Emma had a maid who lived with her. We called her Ma. She was a ward of the state, destitute, and my aunt took her in because she had nowhere else to go. She was not the brightest bulb in the box, but boy, did she ever love the Lord. I never saw her without her Bible, and to see her on her knees anywhere praying was not unusual.

When my aunt Emma died, guess where Ma went to live? That's right, with us. I moved out of my own bedroom and into bunk beds in my brother's room, so she could have a room of her own. And I didn't mind. I had a law on my lens that said, "That's what you do with people who have nowhere else to go." My mother put that law there.

About five years later, after Ma died, my aunt Pearl died (Emma's sister). She was married to my uncle Joe, a retired dentist from New York. He was absolutely lost without my aunt Pearl. Guess where he came to live? You got it, our house. My parents built an addition onto our house for him. Can you imagine the impact that had on me?

My grandmother died shortly after that (my dad's mother). My grandfather was an invalid and needed constant care. It never occurred to my father's family to put him in a nursing home. He went to live with my father's sister. Then he lived with my cousin for a while. Then he came to live with us. He died in a recliner in my living room. Who needs Social Security? Family takes care of family!

When my mother died suddenly at age sixty-six, I spoke at her funeral. Here is what I said about her:

> My mother went for walk with God every day. Where she saw sickness, she healed it; where she saw pain, she comforted it; where she saw hunger, she fed it; where she saw nakedness she clothed it; and where she saw dirt, she cleaned it.

> The Bible tells us that God is love. But the Bible doesn't stop there. It provides instruction about love for each of us.

> First John 3:18 says, "Little children, let us love not in word or speech, but in truth and action." You see, love is a verb. Love is something you do. Love is action. God so loved the world that He *gave* us His Son. God's "love plan" of salvation didn't become real until He put it into action.

> My mother was love in action. The Bible says, "Love your neighbor as yourself." My mother obeyed that command. First John 3:23-24 says, "And this is His commandment, we should believe in the name of His Son Jesus Christ and love one another, just as He has

commanded us. All who obey His commandments abide in Him, and He abides in us, by the Spirit that He has given us."

Everyone in this room can remember a kindness shown to them by my mother. That's just the way she was. Love for her was not something you felt, but something you did.

I never met a less selfish person. She had endless energy, and if you needed something, she was *always* there. She instilled in me a set of values and principles that have guided me well.

If you would remember my mother, don't do it with thought, do it with action. Go out of your way each day to do some kindness for someone. When you do, know that she is pleased.

I began by saying that my mother went for a walk with God every day. Last Sunday when they finished their walk, I think they both realized that they were closer to His house than hers. And I believe God just said, "Ginny Lee, why don't you just come on home with me?"

She was one of a kind, and I was blessed to have her as my mother. She put some of her best laws on my lens, laws that still create results today, laws that are meeting my needs.

Around 1990, Sherrie's mother was getting too old to care for herself. She lived in Seattle and we were in Atlanta. We were worried about her, and we were too far away to do any good. She had been a single mom for over thirty years and raised two wonderful girls all on her own. She was a very independent, self-sufficient woman.

So when I asked Sherrie to see if her mother wanted to come live with us, we weren't sure at all that she would do it. But she surprised us; she was very eager to move in with us.

We finished our basement with a living room, bedroom, and bath so she could have her own little suite and lots of privacy. Sherrie flew to Seattle with her sister, and they put the house up for sale and packed everything up. I flew to Seattle, rented a truck, loaded it with my mother-in-law's belongings, and drove it to Atlanta. I know that that law my mother put on my lens about taking care of family surely had something to do with that.

And as my dad says, "Family is family." When I married Sherrie, I married her family too—kids, mother, and sister, lock, stock, and barrel.

As I said earlier, when Sherrie and I got married, we wrote some of our own vows, and one thing we promised each other was that we would love each other's children as our own. Sherrie's daughter Jennifer was about thirteen or fourteen when Sherrie and I married, and I think she came to love me and trust me. But when she decided to get married, she was conflicted about who should walk her down the aisle. I asked her, "Who do you call Dad?" I think she knew then that I was not that guy. However, she made a wonderful compromise. As she walked down the aisle with her father, she stopped at my row and gave me a huge hug.

Man, I cannot tell you how wonderful that felt. She said a million things to me with that simple hug. At a time when the focus should have been on her, she put it on me. Maybe I've put a good law or two on her lens over the years.

One other thing I'd like to say about Jennifer's wedding was her wedding dress. One of Sherrie's best friends, Anna, was diagnosed with an inoperable brain tumor at age thirty. Anna knew then that she would not be having children of her own, so she gave her wedding dress to Jennifer, and Jennifer wore it at her wedding. At the reception, she did a really neat thing. On a table near the entrance to the reception was a picture of Anna in the dress at her wedding. These words were written on a card next to the picture:

Jennifer's Wedding Dress[17]

The dress was originally worn by Anna, seen here at her wedding in 1986. Anna and Jennifer's mother Sherrie were best friends. In 1990 Anna was diagnosed with an inoperable brain tumor. At that time, knowing she would not have a daughter of her own, Anna gave her wedding dress to Jennifer. Anna died in 1995. Just before, Sherrie and Jennifer were at her side and Jennifer said, "I'm so sorry that you won't see me in the dress at my wedding." Anna faintly whispered back to Jennifer, "Oh, I'll be there." The empty chair at Jennifer's table is simply to acknowledge that, "SHE IS."

These are things that families do. Somehow we have let our culture get away from us. We have adopted laws, and put them on our lenses, and we live as if we hold them as true. Do you see the results you're creating? Are these results going to meet your and society's needs over time? It is time for the pendulum to swing back the other way. We need to change our minds about family.

Let me tell you a cute little story about what I did at my father's funeral. You might wonder why somebody would want to do something "cute" at a funeral. Well, I had a point to make, and afterward some people told me it was cute.

If you've read this far in the book, you know that I'm a Christian and that I believe in heaven. The criteria to get there is, "believe in the Lord Jesus Christ and you will be saved." My dad met that criteria, so I knew exactly where he was and where he'll always be.

At funerals we always talk about the deceased in the past tense. Well, to me, my dad was more alive at the funeral than he'd ever been in his life. And I wanted the mourners to know that. The body lying in the casket wasn't my father (even though the casket was closed). That was just the thing that housed my dad while he was in *this* life.

So I got up to speak. I said a few words about my dad, and then my cell phone rang. I acted really embarrassed, apologizing to the audience for it.

But then I took the phone out of my pocket and answered it. Isn't that cute? As instructed, my niece in the front row had called my cell phone right on cue. So when I answered the phone, I said, "Hello?" I waited a second and then I said, "Is that you, Dad?" Then I proceeded to have a ten-minute conversation with him. The message was clear: he was alive. And I wanted everyone to know that.

My dad, the family man, is alive and well. And if he had the power to change anything about our culture today, it would be to reestablish the role of family.

Henri Nouween said, "A life is like a day; it goes by so fast. If I am careless with my days, how can I be careful with my life? It finally boils down to a question of deep and strong conviction. When I am truly convinced that preparing my heart is more important than preparing the Christmas tree, then I will be a lot less frustrated at the end of the day."

Deep and strong convictions are the laws that are on your lens. You need deep and strong convictions about preparing your heart for your family.

Let me close this chapter with a poem. It tells us why we need to change the laws on our lens about family.

THE BRIDGE BUILDER[18]

> An old man going down a lone highway
> Came in the evening cold and gray
> To a chasm vast and deep and wide
> Through which was flowing a sullen tide.
> The old man crossed in the twilight dim;
> That swollen stream held no fears for him;

So he turned when safe on the other side
And built a bridge to span the tide.
"Old man," said a fellow pilgrim near,
"You are wasting your strength with building here;
Your journey will end with the ending day;
You never again must pass this way;
You have crossed the chasm deep and wide,
Why build this bridge at the evening tide?"

The builder lifted his old gray head
"Good friend, in the path I have come," he said,
"There follows after me today
A youth whose feet must pass this way.
This swollen stream which was naught to me
To that fair-haired youth may a pitfall be;
He, too, must cross in the twilight dim;
Good friend, I'm building this bridge for him."

We need to build bridges today for our grandchildren. We can start with showing them the importance of family. It's up to us to save our families— one law at a time.

14

Group Think

As we saw in an earlier chapter, businesses, like individuals, have laws on their lenses. So do special interest groups, clubs, gangs, and organizations. This might also be referred to as *group mentality*. Let's take a look at some of these and explore their laws.

Kiwanis[19]

Kiwanis was founded in 1915 in Detroit, Michigan, and was originally focused on business networking. Since then their focus has shifted to service, primarily to young children. In addition, they have gone international, and they have opened their membership to women. Today, Kiwanis clubs are in eighty countries, and each local club serves the children in its community uniquely.

There are approximately 250,000 members of Kiwanis today, and they stage nearly 150,000 projects each year and raise over $100 million annually. In June 2010, Kiwanis announced the Eliminate Project in conjunction with UNICEF, which aims to save 129 million mothers and their babies from tetanus by 2015.

Kiwanis has six permanent objectives. Through the decades these tenets have remained unchanged, and they represent the laws on the lens of

Kiwanis International. By joining a Kiwanis Club, you are in effect signing up to put these laws on your lens as well, and to think accordingly.

- To give primacy to the human and spiritual, rather than to the material values of life
- To encourage the daily living of the golden rule in all human relationships
- To promote the adoption and the application of higher social, business, and professional standards
- To develop, by precept and example, a more intelligent, aggressive, and serviceable citizenship
- To provide a practical means to form enduring friendships, to render altruistic service, and to build better communities
- To cooperate in creating and maintaining that sound public opinion and high idealism which make possible the increase of righteousness, justice, patriotism, and goodwill

When you have laws like these on your lens, it drives what you do. And those actions will create results that should not only meet your needs, but also the needs of the world.

Ku Klux Klan (KKK)[20]

Now let's contrast the belief system of Kiwanis with that of the KKK. The Klan, as it is commonly known today, is a far-right organization in the United States. It advocates extremist, reactionary positions, such as white supremacy, white nationalism, and anti-immigration, historically expressed through terrorism. Since the mid-twentieth century, the Klan has also been anti-communist, and in its current manifestation is splintered into several chapters, all classified as hate groups.

The first Klan adopted white costumes: robes, masks, and conical hats, designed to be outlandish and terrifying, and to hide the identities of members. The second Klan flourished nationwide in the early and mid-

1920s and adopted the same costumes and code words as the first Klan while introducing cross burnings. The third Klan emerged after World War II and was associated with opposing the civil rights movement and progress among minorities. All incarnations of the Klan have well-established records of engaging in terrorism.

Once African Americans secured federal legislation to protect their civil and voting rights, the Klan shifted its focus to opposing court-ordered busing to desegregate schools, affirmative action, and more open immigration. In 1971, Klan members used bombs to destroy ten school buses in Pontiac, Michigan.

In 1995, Don Black began a small bulletin board system on the Internet called Stormfront. Today, Stormfront has become a prominent online forum for white nationalism, Neo-Nazism, hate speech, racism, and anti-Semitism.

The modern KKK is not one organization, but rather it is composed of small independent chapters across the United States. Estimates are that about two-thirds of KKK members are concentrated in the southern United States. Membership in the Klan today is not large, and is estimated to be between 5,000 and 8,000 members across 179 chapters. Many Klan groups have formed strong alliances with other white supremacist groups, such as neo-Nazis, adopting the look and emblems of white power skinheads.

Interestingly enough, the ACLU has provided legal support to the Klan in defense of its First Amendment rights to hold public rallies, parades, and marches, as well as its right to field political candidates.

Current Klan splinter divisions have grown substantially since the 2008 election of President Barack Obama, the first African American to hold that office. Ex-Grand Wizard David Duke has claimed that thousands of Tea Party movement activists have urged him to run for president in 2012, and at the time of this writing, he is seriously considering entering the Republican Party primaries.

Since it is a hate organization, joining the Klan speaks volumes about the laws on your lens about African Americans, immigrants, and Jews. When your view of the world is through a lens with these types of laws, your actions become very predictable, as well as the results they'll create.

What need is probably driving laws like that? I think it is esteem and self-importance. The only thing that separates a Klansman from a black man is the color of his skin. So, the only thing he can do to differentiate himself is to believe that the color of his skin makes him better. With a law like that, what is a Klansman likely to feel when he sees a black man with a white woman? Rage. Then what is he likely to do? Anything cowardly—like burning a cross in the black man's front yard at night while wearing a hood. The results are predictable and not likely to meet anybody's needs.

Rotary Club[21]

The Rotary Club was founded in 1905 by attorney Paul Harris and his colleague Sylvester Schiele. The early members chose the name Rotary, because initially they rotated subsequent weekly club meetings to one another's offices. Rotary is now an international organization.

The stated purpose of the organization is to bring together business and professional leaders to:

- Provide humanitarian service
- Encourage high ethical standards in all vocations
- Help build goodwill and peace in the world

It is a secular organization open to all persons regardless of race, color, creed, gender, or political preference. There are approximately 34,000 clubs and over 1.22 million members worldwide. The members of Rotary Clubs are known as Rotarians, and members usually meet weekly for breakfast, lunch, or dinner. These are social events as well as opportunities to organize work on their service goals. Rotary Clubs have two mottos:

- Service above self.
- They profit most who serve best.

The objectives of Rotary are to encourage and foster the ideal of service as a basis of worthy enterprise; and, in particular, to encourage and foster four objectives:

- The development of acquaintance as an opportunity for service
- High ethical standards in business and professions, the recognition of the worthiness of all useful occupations, and the dignifying of each Rotarian's occupation as an opportunity to serve society
- The application of the ideal of service in each Rotarian's personal, business, and community life
- The advancement of international understanding, goodwill, and peace through a world fellowship of business and professional persons united in the ideal of service

These objectives are set against the Rotary Four-Way Test, used to see if a planned action is compatible with the Rotarian spirit. The test was developed as a set of guidelines for restoring faltering businesses and was adopted as the standard of ethics by Rotary in 1942. It is still seen as a standard for ethics in business management:

- Is it the truth?
- Is it fair to all concerned?
- Will it build goodwill and better friendships?
- Will it be beneficial to all concerned?

In 1985, Rotary launched its PolioPlus program to immunize all of the world's children against polio. In 2005, Rotary claimed to have contributed half a billion dollars to the cause, resulting in the immunization of nearly two billion children worldwide.

As of 2006, the Rotary Club is in over 200 countries, making it the largest club in the world based on number of branches, and second largest based on membership, behind Lions Club International.

The laws on the lenses of Rotarians are about truth, fairness, and goodwill, which benefit everyone. As you process life as it comes at you at one hundred miles per hour, laws like these will drive everything you do in a positive way. When you join Rotary, you sign up for these laws. What will you feel when things in life occur for you that are unfair or not the truth? Resentment or rejection. How will this affect your actions? You'll refrain from doing what you should. Are truth and fairness and goodwill going to create results that will meet your needs over time? My guess is yes.

Street Gangs

Again, let's contrast the laws on the lenses of Rotarians with the laws on the lenses of members of street gangs. Sociologists as well as gang members have isolated the following reasons for joining a street gang:

- Identity
- Recognition
- Belonging
- Love
- Discipline
- Money

The reason that young people seek these things from gangs is because they're not finding them elsewhere in their lives. Feelings of fear, hatred, bigotry, poverty, disenfranchisement, and the general breakdown of social values are also considered motivations for joining a gang.

The criminal activities of gangs are virtually limitless, but certainly include things like intimidation, harassment, vandalism, criminal trespass, sexual

96

assault, weapons violations, kidnapping, murder, murder for hire, violence against law enforcement, and drugs for both sale and possession.

The six major components of gang culture can be summarized as follows:[22]

Reputation—This is paramount to gang members. Their reputation extends not only to each individual, but to the gang as a whole. Gang members brag about crimes and usually bend reality in their stories to increase their sense of power.

Respect—Every gang member wants respect. And they will do just about anything to get it. Beyond the individual, they want respect for the gang, their family, their territory, and any other aspect of their lives that fall within their circle of influence. Being respected is being feared. Respect is based on a reputation for being violent and dangerous.

Disrespect for Rivals—The biggest way to gain respect is by demonstrating disrespect, disdain, and lack of fear of rivals. The more a gang member displays this attitude, the more recognized he or she will be within the gang.

Retaliation/Revenge—In gangs, no challenge goes unanswered. No act of disrespect passes without retaliation. Many times drive-by shootings are a result of a gang member feeling disrespected. As they say in the gang, "Today's witness is tomorrow's suspect, and is the next day's victim."

Consequences as a Right of Passage—Most gang members realize that gang life eventually results in some form of grief and suffering. Therefore, young members are often not fully recognized and given status as full members until they have suffered the consequences of gang life—injury, incarceration, or the death of a family member through violence.

Problems Handled from Within—Disagreement among gang members is generally handled without any involvement from police. Even rival gangs will refuse to testify against each other. Participating in the legal system at any level is seen as weakness.

Disregard for the Rights of Nonmembers—Gang members never show any sympathy toward nonmembers. It is a sign of weakness and reflects poorly on the gang member's reputation. In private it is different, but in public, expressions of sympathy are not tolerated.

Gang activity affects our communities in many ways:

- Increased crime
- Increased cost for police services
- Increased cost for security services for businesses and schools
- Increased burden on social services for businesses and schools
- Increased burden on social service systems and emergency and hospital systems
- Negative impact on business recruitment, overall city economic development, and overall city image
- Increased trauma, grief, confusion, and depression over the injury and death of a loved one because of gang violence
- Increased likelihood that you will become a victim of crime or that your personal property will be damaged through acts of vandalism
- Increased fear for your personal safety, the safety of your family or your neighborhood
- May cause you to become a victim of harassment and intimidation or other more violent crimes, such as a drive-by shooting

The core values of gang members shape the way they see the world and become the laws on their lens. These laws look something like this:

- My reputation defines who I am, and it must be protected at all times by any measure necessary.
- Everyone must show me respect, and those who don't will suffer the consequences.
- All acts of disrespect, real or perceived, must be met with violent retaliation.
- Physical harm, prison, and the possible loss of life are inevitable, and I accept that possibility as a member.
- You don't snitch, even against a rival gang. Lying is always a better choice.
- If you aren't in my gang, you deserve no respect from me.
- Violent acts mean approval.

I can't even imagine what it must be like to see the world this way. Yet with laws like these, gang member behavior is very predictable. We should not wonder why they do the things that they do. And the results they create are really a self-fulfilling prophecy of physical injuries, prison, or death.

Other Groups[23]

There are so many different types of groups, organizations, clubs, associations, societies, and so on. Just a few of these entities are listed below:

<u>Lions Club</u>—a secular service organization with over 44,500 clubs and more than 1.3 million members in 206 countries around the world. Headquartered in Oakbrook, Illinois, the organization aims to meet the needs of communities on a local and global scale.

<u>American Legion</u>—was chartered and incorporated by Congress in 1919 as a patriotic veterans organization devoted to mutual helpfulness. It is the nation's largest veteran's service organization, committed to mentoring and sponsorship of youth programs in our communities, advocating patriotism and honor, promoting a strong national security, and continued devotion to its fellow service members and veterans.

Shriners—established in 1870 and based in the United States. It is a fraternity based on fun, fellowship, and the principles of brotherly love, relief, and truth. The organization is best known for the Shriners Hospitals for Children.

American Association of Retired Persons (AARP)—is a nonprofit, nonpartisan membership organization for people age fifty and over, with forty million members. It is dedicated to enhancing the quality of life for members as they age. They deliver value to members through information, advocacy, and service. AARP also provides a wide range of unique benefits, special products, and services for its members.

Gentlemen's Clubs—most of these types of clubs are identified with female nudity, and they always exploit women in some way or another.

Alcoholics Anonymous (AA)—is an international mutual aid organization whose primary purpose is to keep members sober and help other alcoholics achieve sobriety. AA was founded in 1935 by Bill Wilson and Dr. Bob Smith and now claims two million members. It is known for its Twelve Step program of spiritual and character development.

National Rifle Association (NRA)—an organization of 4.3 million members that defends and fosters the Second Amendment rights of all law-abiding Americans. The NRA promotes firearms and hunting safety, enhanced marksmanship, sport shooting, and educating of the general public about firearms in their historic, technological, and artistic context.

Mothers against Drunk Driving (MADD)—was incorporated on September 5, 1980. The mission of MADD is to stop drunk driving, support the victims of this violent crime, and prevent underage drinking. To date, MADD claims to have saved nearly 300,000 lives.

Gender Clubs—These types of clubs limit their membership to only one gender. Examples are the Boy Scouts of America and the Girl Scouts of the

USA, and the Augusta National Golf Club in Augusta, Georgia. Augusta National has only 300 members, which includes black members, but no females.

The Humane Society of the United States—is the nation's largest animal protection organization, backed by eleven million Americans. Its aim is to reduce suffering and improve the lives of all animals by advocating for better laws, investigating animal cruelty, encouraging corporations to adopt animal-friendly policies, conducting animal rescue and emergency response, and by providing direct care for thousands of animals at sanctuaries, emergency shelters, wildlife rehabilitation centers, and mobile veterinary clinics.

UNICEF—is a children's organization operating in over 190 countries. UNICEF believes that the nurturing and caring for children is the cornerstone of human progress. It works with communities to overcome the obstacles that poverty, violence, disease, and discrimination place in a child's path. It believes that its mission will advance the cause of humanity.

US Marine Corps—is a military organization, a branch of the United States Navy. There about 250,000 active and reserve marines. They advertise themselves as "The Few. The Proud. The Marines." The Marine Corps makes three commitments: to make marines, to win our nation's battles, and to develop quality citizens. They also serve three entities— God, Corps, and Country. Their mantra is Semper Fidelis (always faithful).

There are certainly many more examples of groups in all sizes, shapes, and missions. Each of these groups has a unique set of laws on their lenses that they want members to adopt when they join. So you must choose carefully to be sure the group you choose represents laws that are compatible with your own. Once you identify yourself with their laws, life will occur for you as those laws dictate.

All groups have a mission, a vision, a code of conduct, a reason for being, a purpose, a goal, a set of objectives, a modus operandi, and a way of operating. How do these components compare with yours? If they compare well, then you can examine the group's results over time and decide whether the group will meet your needs over time as well. If not, you probably don't want to be a member of this group.

15

John Lennon Was Right After All

What a challenge it is to write about love. It is a most difficult word to get your head around. In English, the word *love* can refer to a variety of different feelings, states, and attitudes, ranging from generic pleasure (I love ice cream) to intense interpersonal pleasure (I love my wife). Love can be an emotion of strong personal attachment, and love can be a virtue representing all human kindness, compassion, and affection. Love is central to many religions, as in "God is love."

Love is both a noun and a verb. It can be something you feel as well as something you do. Love is sometimes used interchangeably with sexual intercourse, as in "we made love." Love can be family oriented, such as emotional closeness to family; it can be platonic, as in friendships; and it can be religious, as in profound oneness with God.

Love in its various forms acts as a major facilitator of interpersonal relationships and, because of its central psychological importance, it is one of the most common themes in the arts. At the same time, science defines love as an evolved state of survival instinct, primarily used to facilitate the continuation of the species through reproduction. This diversity of uses and meanings, combined with the complexity of feelings involved, makes love unusually difficult to consistently define.

We can have love for things like clothes, cars, jewelry, houses, or food. But that kind of love is different from the love we have for people. Even within the people category, the love we have for a parent, child, spouse, family member, or friend are all very different from one another. We can also have love for intangibles like our jobs or our looks; and for activities like baseball, gardening, or reading.

Love is not to be confused with lust. Lust is only a physical thing and a great imposter. For our purposes in this chapter, I want to focus only on the aspect of love that exists between people and with God.

I believe that the *action* of love creates the blissful *feeling* with the same name, and that when the action stops, the blissful feeling goes away. I believe that everyone is capable of loving and of being loved. I also believe that the opposite of love is not hate, but fear, which can generate hate, greed, or jealousy. You cannot love and fear at the same time. Consider love to be the base of the pyramid in all your relationships, the base upon which you can build other things.

You have to start by loving yourself. And I don't mean this in a narcissistic way, but as an acceptance of yourself. You have to have congruence between what you believe and what you do in order to see yourself as lovable. If you can't honestly see yourself as lovable, then you will have trouble giving or receiving love from others.

I have observed couples whom I consider to be truly in love, as evidenced by their staying together for decades. The major characteristic I see is action, not simply feeling. Some of the things I have observed these couples doing are:

- They do things for the other person even when they don't feel like it.
- They go out of their way to do things to make others happy or just feel good.
- They allow the other person space to do his or her thing.

- They do not insist on getting their own way.
- All their actions are courteous and considerate.
- They look out for the other's interests.
- They control their anger toward each other.
- They take no pleasure in the other's disappointments.
- They have complete trust in each other.
- Their love is unconditional.
- They look toward the future together, beyond their current circumstances, with hope and anticipation.

My personal advice to you about love is this:

- Never ask for love, just give it. Expect nothing in return. Therefore, when you receive love, you will know immediately that it is something the other person wanted to give you.
- Never force love. It will come to you if you can risk giving it away without expectation.
- Say "I love you" often and mean it, and show it through your actions.
- Always put yourself in the other person's shoes and try to see things from his or her perspective.
- Make your love unconditional. If it isn't, it isn't really love but some form of opportunism on your part.
- Realize that you can lose love and never take it for granted.
- If you love you will eventually get hurt. Love anyway.

As a Christian, the ultimate authority on love for me is the Bible. Interestingly enough, the Bible has a lot to say about love. It teaches that love came from God because God *is* love. Being created in His image, we are endowed with the capacity to love and be loved. According to the Bible, love is caring in action. It is not something we feel, but something we do.

God's love for us is unconditional. He sent His Son to die for humanity, impartially and for everyone. Unfortunately, our love is usually conditional and based on how other people behave toward us.

Probably the most familiar scripture about love in the Bible is the thirteenth chapter of First Corinthians. It seems to be read at every wedding I've attended. In this chapter, the apostle Paul tells us sixteen things about God's perspective on what love is and what love is not. Paul says:

- Love is patient. Love doesn't rush people into relationship, it gives them the time they need. When a compromise is called for, love waits patiently. When children don't learn as fast as they might, love repeats things with patience. Love allows people to take the time they need.

- Love is kind. Love isn't condescending or obtuse, and it doesn't talk behind your back. Love is sensitive to the feelings of others, is courteous, and is never sarcastic.

- Loves keeps no record of wrongs. Love doesn't have a scorecard— for good things or bad things. Keeping no record implies keeping no memory. I think true love really forgets wrongs.

- Love rejoices in the truth. Regardless of the consequences, love rejoices in truth. Sometimes truth is painful for us or for our families, but love always rejoices in truth. Remember also that truth is a person. Jesus said, "I am the way, the truth, and the life."

- Love always protects. Love doesn't want anyone to get hurt, physically or emotionally. Love stands in the gap for others and protects them.

- Love always trusts. Always. Not sometimes, not when it's convenient, not when it's earned or warranted, but *always*. My father asked me one time if I knew how to make a man trustworthy? I said I didn't know. He said simply, "You trust him."

- Love always hopes. Love is always looking forward to something, always sees a better tomorrow. Loves sees the glass as half full, not half empty.

- Love always perseveres. Love never gives up—*never*. Love always wants another try, love is not a quitter. Love can persevere because it always has hope.

- Love does not envy. Love doesn't want what you have, but is happy for you that you have it. Love is assured and comfortable and doesn't need anything else.
- Love does not boast. Because love is comfortable with itself, it doesn't need to brag. Love is transparent; it lets you see who the other person really is, so no bragging is ever required.
- Love is not proud. Love never partakes in outward acts of self-importance. Love is comfortable in its own skin.
- Love is not rude. Love is courteous, considerate, caring about the feelings of others. To be rude implies a focus on self. Love focuses on others.
- Love is not self-seeking. Love looks out for you, not itself. Love wants you to have whatever you need, even if it means it has to go without.
- Love is not easily angered. Since love is patient, it is very slow to anger. Love gives the benefit of the doubt to others.
- Love does not delight in evil. Love never wants to see bad things happen to people. Love doesn't want revenge or retaliation; love wants goodness.
- Love never fails. This is much more than perseverance. It really means that love cannot fail. Think about that. *Love cannot fail.* The reason is that God is love and He can never fail.

Paul goes on to tell us how important love is to God. He says that if we could speak every language, but didn't have love, we would only be like a clanging cymbal. If we could predict the future, knew the answer to every mystery, had all knowledge, and had faith that could move mountains, but didn't have love, we would be nothing! If we gave everything we had to the poor and were willing to die, but didn't have love, we would gain nothing in God's sight.

God certainly places a high importance on love. Loves comes from the heart. Solomon said in the book of Proverbs, "Above all else, guard your heart, for it is the wellspring of life." Then Jesus said, "Store up treasure in heaven, for where your treasure is, there will your heart be also." Our hearts, and the love that emanates from them, are of paramount importance to God. In fact, Jesus said that all the laws of the Old Testament could be summarized in two statements:

- Love the Lord with all your heart, soul, and mind.
- Love your neighbor as yourself.

That's it. All the laws in the Old Testament summed up in two statements about love. Pretty incredible!

Okay, so where is the discussion about the laws on our lenses about love? We all have those laws. All the things I've discussed in this chapter are laws that I believe. If you put these laws on your lens, I believe you will create the best results for yourself over time. However, there are an endless number of laws about love that exist on people's lenses that have no chance of meeting their needs over time. Here are just a few:

- Love hurts, I won't do it anymore.
- It didn't work for Mom and Dad, so I'm not doing it either.
- Loving someone makes me too vulnerable.
- You have to earn my love.
- Saying "I love you" isn't very manly.
- I give love to the same degree I get it.
- When I love, I expect something in return.
- I don't need love. Enough girls sleep with me without it.
- When I'm angry with someone, the love stops right there.
- You have to love me first.
- Love is overrated; I don't need it.
- I've been married so long, I don't need to tell my spouse I love him/her anymore.
- I just assume they know I love them.

Have you heard any of these before? I'm sure you have, and probably many others. One of the five basic human needs is love. With bad laws on your lens, your need *to love and be loved* will never get met. With bad laws on your lens, you can never create results that will meet your need for love. Examine yourself. Have the courage to change your laws. Change your mind. Create better results for yourself. John Lennon may have been right after all: *All You Need Is Love.*

16

Who Works for Whom Here?

There has been a lot in the news in the past few years about the unemployment rate in America and our tremendous national debt. While President Bush started spending money that we didn't have, President Obama has taken it to another level, to where now we have over $14 trillion in national debt. The mortgage crisis certainly contributed to the downturn in our economy, as well as many other factors. The foreclosure rate on homes in America has never been higher. And today, unemployment is hovering around 9 percent nationally, and is even higher in some places, like Detroit. Employers are sitting on capital, afraid to invest because of so much uncertainty. Given all this background, is it any wonder that employers and employees are insecure?

Unemployment[24]

As of April 2011, there were 112 metropolitan areas in America with unemployment rates at 10 percent, and six states with unemployment over 10 percent.

- Nevada   12.5%
- California   11.9 %
- Rhode Island   10.9%
- Florida   10.8%
- Michigan   10.2%

- Mississippi   10.4%
- South Carolina   10.0%

And in Puerto Rico, the unemployment rate is a whopping 16 percent.

Foreclosures[25]

If you are a homeowner and unemployed, the likelihood of foreclosure is high. If you have a job but are already in foreclosure, then the stress in your life is equally high. The four big stress categories are: in foreclosure, near foreclosure, unemployed, and near unemployed (that is, worried about keeping your job). Some people fall in multiple categories. Let me share a few statistics with you from the Mortgage Bankers Association that quantify the magnitude of the foreclosure problem in America:

- One out of every two hundred homes will be foreclosed upon. If you live in a neighborhood with six hundred homes, then three of your neighbors are in foreclosure.
- Every three months, one-quarter of a million new families enter into foreclosure.
- One child in every classroom in America is at risk of losing his or her home because his or her parents can't pay the mortgage.
- Falling home prices do not allow many families facing foreclosure to refinance.

We have this foreclosure problem in America because of the laws on the lenses of both borrowers and lenders. The laws on the lenses of mortgage lenders used to be:

- The borrower had to have a job.
- The borrower's income had to be sufficient to make the mortgage payments.
- The borrower had to be credit worthy.
- The borrower had to put 20 percent down in cash.

However, the lenders got greedy and began to view their lending criteria as too strict. They thought, "Just think how much more money we could make if we lowered our standards." So they changed the laws on their lenses and started lending money to people to buy houses, even though those people really had no realistic way of paying back the loan. The results were predictable. Do you think those results met their needs over time? Not even a short time.

Borrowers were no better than lenders. Borrowers had similar laws on their lenses as the lenders did when it came to borrowing standards. But when borrowers saw that lenders had lowered the lending criteria, the borrowers then changed the law on their lenses. Their law now said, "I can afford to buy a much bigger house now." So the borrowers began to borrow more money than they could afford to pay back. Everybody felt good about it. Lenders had money and wanted people to borrow it. Borrowers wanted more from life, so they were grateful to take the money. No pun intended, but it was a house of cards. The results were predictable. And in a few short years, it was clear that no one's needs were being met. Lenders went under, banks got bailed out, and consumers started losing their homes to foreclosure.

The foreclosure experience is traumatic. When homeowners are foreclosed upon, over 70 percent feel scared or depressed. This increases stress.

Many people today are in a sad financial state, and are already at their financial edge. Consider that:[26]

- Forty-three percent of American households spend more than they earn each year.
- Fifty-two percent of all employees live paycheck to paycheck.
- Forty-two percent of American households do not have enough liquid assets to support themselves for three months.
- Forty-six percent of American households have less than five thousand dollars in liquid assets, including IRAs.

The tipping point for people entering foreclosure is usually caused by one of the following scenarios:[26]

- Thirty-two percent lose their job.
- Twenty-five percent have a health crisis.
- Eighty-five percent have already missed one mortgage payment.
- Fifty percent have missed two mortgage payments.
- Most have no savings, no available credit, and no family with money.
- Most are first-time buyers and their mortgage is less than three years old.
- They have already refinanced two or three times.

Americans are in tough financial times. Unemployment is high; foreclosures are rampant; health care costs continue to escalate; and we're now paying well over three dollars a gallon for gasoline, which causes other prices—such as food prices—to increase as well. Add to that many seniors who are on fixed incomes and worried about the future of Social Security and Medicare, and it is clear that Americans have a lot to be stressed about.

Employers

Employers are afraid of a business slowdown and are conserving their cash. They are watching their expenses like hawks. The cost of employee benefits is rising, because health care costs keep rising. Employers are watching all their discretionary spending and are reducing or eliminating things like training, travel, attending conventions or conferences, and consulting. And who can blame them? Expansion plans are being put on hold, and the pervasive attitude is wait and see.

As a result of all this, what kind of laws are employers putting on their lenses?

- We just can't give salary increases this year.
- We're not hiring until things seem more certain.

- I am mandating a 25 percent reduction in all expenses.
- We need to cut 10 percent of our staff.
- Our people are just going to need to work more hours.
- Our employees should feel lucky that they have this job.
- We're going to need to close this business down soon.
- We might need to cheat a little on our taxes this year.
- We need to raise our prices right now.
- We need to start charging for the things we used to do for free.
- We need to take money from the employee retirement accounts.
- Let's start fudging those invoices a little. Customers won't notice.
- We're not going to pay our bills until they're ninety days old.

Have you heard employers starting to talk this way? They are just as afraid as employees. They have mortgages, too, and may also be facing a foreclosure. Stress and fear will cause people to put different laws on their lenses. And those new laws will certainly create different results. The question employers need to ask themselves is, will these new laws meet my needs over time? I'm not saying that in bad economic times businesses don't need to behave differently. They do. But when the tough times are over, employers need to be sure that a necessary but temporary law doesn't become permanent.

Employees

Now let's take a minute and look at the financial state of America from the eyes of the employee. Any employee today absolutely needs to keep his or her job. Many employees live in fear of losing their jobs. They know that if they lose their jobs, the next thing they'll lose will be their house or their car. Stress like this causes people to change laws on their lenses. What about the employee who had a law that said, "I treat everyone with respect," but later that week finds out that the company is eliminating two of the ten positions at his level? He might consider changing that law to say, "I need this job and I'll discredit my coworker in order to keep it." Do you believe that could happen in an environment such as America is in today? You better believe it could. And more just like it, some of which might even include violence.

For many years when I was an employee, I had a law on my lens that said, "I'm overpaid, just not enough." In other words, I wanted more money but less work. It did not create the results I wanted and it never met my needs, not even in the short term.

But I imagine some employees today have laws that keep them from realizing their full potential:

- My boss hates me.
- My life will be great when my boss leaves or gets fired.
- I always do as little as possible to get by.
- I deserve that promotion and I'll do anything to get it.
- They wouldn't dare fire me. I've been here twenty years.
- I only steal small amounts of office supplies.
- I only pad my expense account because my pay is so low.
- I don't know who they think they are, but I'm entitled to this job.
- If I lose this job, I'll lose my house.
- I need to make myself invaluable to this company to protect my job.
- If I lose this job, I'll have to start robbing banks.

As crazy as it may seem, there are employees with these laws, and many others, on their lenses.

There are also many people in America today who have given up even looking for a job. Many who are on welfare, disability, and food stamps may not even *want* a job. Over time, entitlement programs will create an even greater financial burden on those that do work.

The stress created by the current financial situation in our country is forcing people to think things they wouldn't ordinarily think. When people get desperate, that's what they do. The need driving these law changes is their need to live. No doubt about it. And with desperate laws come desperate actions and desperate results. Examine yourself and make sure that you are in your right mind.

17

I Love My Car but
I Don't Know Why

The automobile is one of several inventions that have transformed America. The first black Ford that rolled off Henry Ford's assembly line in 1896 was the beginning of one of America's largest and longest-lasting industries. In 2007, there were over 250 million cars registered in America, more than any other country.[27] Virtually every person that is of driving age has a car.

I have also heard, though I can't confirm it, that one out of every five people employed today in America has a job related to the auto industry. This includes not only the autoworkers at manufacturing plants, but also all the things that go on cars, like tires, radios, mirrors, leather, plastic, batteries, paint, and on and on. Other jobs related to the auto industry include road construction and maintenance, oil and gas production, policemen, insurance companies, repair shops, and the Department of Motor Vehicles. There are many others, too numerous to list.

Laws about Cars

For most Americans a car is a necessity—to get to work or school, to go to the grocery store, to run any necessary errands. Today, cars come in all shapes and sizes, colors and models. We have sedans, station wagons, hatchbacks, trucks, minivans, SUVs, convertibles, and sports cars. There is a car for everybody.

When the first car was sold, what laws about cars do you think were on the lens of the buyer? I'm sure it had something to do with fun, experimentation, novelty, and maybe even impressing others. Remember, there weren't many roads or even gas stations. Contrast the simplicity of how we thought about the car one hundred years ago to the way we think about it today.

Today cars are status symbols to some, but just practical transportation to others. For some people cars are an extension of who they are. Their cars define them. As a result, they will spend enormous amounts of money on their cars. For someone with a law on his or her lens that says, "My car defines me," how much do you think he or she will spend on a car? Right, a lot. If that person also has a law on his or her lens that says "European cars are the best," what type of car do you think he or she will drive? Sure, he or she will drive a BMW or Mercedes, or something else from Europe. Remember, these laws determine what we think. That in turn drives what we feel and what we do. Our behavior becomes very predictable.

For some people, cars are a huge blind spot. While those car fanatics make rational decisions in other aspects of their life, they make irrational decisions when it comes to their cars. There are people out there with car payments greater than their rent or mortgage payments. Some people live paycheck to paycheck and don't have enough left over each month to save even five dollars, because their car payments are so high.

Cost

The cost of operating a car today is significant. After the cost of the car, there is insurance, tags, repairs, cleaning, and ordinary maintenance—like tires and windshield wipers, and gasoline to run it. It adds up. One of the worst things about the cost of owning a car is that it is an asset that depreciates rather than appreciates. If you pay $35,000 for your car, in five years it will probably be worth less than half its original value. Contrast that to a house that costs $300,000. In five years it might be worth $350,000 (except for the recent mortgage fiasco, during which housing values have uncharacteristically declined as well).

The cost of gasoline today, in the latter half of 2011, is right around $3.60 per gallon. There is great pressure on the government to lower America's dependence on fossil fuels, particularly foreign oil. People are demanding cars with better gas mileage, while others are pushing for alternative forms of energy for cars. There is uncertainty about the future.

Safety Laws

There were very few traffic laws one hundred years ago, whereas today you practically need a master's degree to pass a driving exam. The safety laws of drivers one hundred years ago were probably very simple: don't go too fast and don't crash. Today we have laws not only about speed, but also about seat belts, car seats, air bags, school buses, fire hydrants, and traveling safe distances from other cars.

Do you see how the laws on our lenses regarding cars have changed over the years? Whereas we used to think of cars as a luxury, today we think of them as a necessity. Where we used to think of them as only practical, today we think of them as status symbols; and some people see them as a possession that defines them as a person. Whereas we used to think about cars as something we would keep forever, today we think about getting another car every two or three years. The need that drives laws like these is self-esteem or the need to feel important.

18

I Ain't Much for Book Learnin'

One of the most important things for a successful and rewarding life is a good education. Today it is estimated that there are over seventy-five million students in the United States, from kindergarten through graduate school.[28]

When our country first began, right after the Revolutionary War, the education that people received came almost exclusively from their parents in the home. As the country grew, communities built small schools for the needs of their children. Then, of course, it grew to county schools and state colleges. Later the federal government began subsidizing the states' costs for education. The federal budget for education submitted to Congress in 2011 is $78 billion.[29] This includes $35 billion in Pell Grants, which are essentially student loans that don't have to be repaid. Education in America has become big business.

Somewhere along the way, the law on our lenses changed from, "Education is a local responsibility" to "Education is a federal government responsibility." Parents who once had a law on their lens that said, "Sex education should be taught at home" changed to "Schools should teach my kids about sex," or "The government should do it." In fact, today there are some who believe condoms should be issued by the schools. How did we get here? More and more parents are abdicating their responsibilities to the school system. Are the results going to meet our needs? America's academic test scores would suggest not.

Quality

At one time American schools were considered the best in the world. Today we aren't even in the top ten. The top sixteen countries in math and science scores are as follows: [30]

1. Singapore
2. Taiwan
3. South Korea
4. Japan
5. Hong Kong
6. Hungary
7. England
8. Czech Republic
9. Russia
10. Slovenia
11. United States
12. Lithuania
13. Australia
14. Sweden
15. Armenia
16. Italy

This study is called Trends in International Math and Science Study (TIMSS), and it involved a half million students from forty-one countries. In short, the tests showed American fourth-graders performing poorly, middle school students performing worse, and high school students were basically unable to compete. By the same criteria that used to say we were average in elementary school, we appear to be near the bottom at the high school level. For those of you who don't think this picture applies to your school, chances are that even if your school compares well in SAT scores, it will still be a lightweight on the international scale.

You would think that with our vastly superior resources and the level of spending on education, which far exceeds other countries, we would outperform nearly everyone. Not so. The cause for the failure appears to be weak math and science curricula in United States middle schools. In middle school, most countries shift curricula from basic arithmetic and elementary science in the direction of chemistry, physics, algebra, and geometry. Even poor countries generally teach a half year of algebra and a half year of geometry to every eighth grader. In US middle schools, however, most students continue to review arithmetic. And they are more likely to study earth science and life science, rather than physics or chemistry.

Our teachers and our textbooks seem to be lacking when compared to those of other countries. According to Pascal Forgione Jr., PhD and United States Commissioner of Education Statistics, "Our schools systematically let our kids down. By grade four American students only score in the middle of twenty-six countries reported. By grade eight they are in the bottom third, and at the finish line where it really counts we're near dead last. It's even worse when you notice that some of the superior countries in grade eight (especially the Asians) were not even included in published twelfth grade results because they do not need twelve grades."[31]

Somewhere along the line, the law on our collective lenses shifted from "education is important" to "we don't care about education." The irony is that we spend billions on education and we still score low. Something is broken.

Of course, there are many different views on education in America. Teachers and school administrators have a view, parents and PTOs have a view, legislators who fund schools have a view, and certainly students have a view. Each has a unique set of laws on their lenses, depending on their perspective. And of course, what we pay teachers doesn't necessarily help our dilemma.

One of the biggest changes in the law on our lenses is safety in the schools. The tragedy at Columbine High School in April of 1999 changed all the rules. Now metal detectors are commonplace in many schools. Our kids are exposed to everything imaginable in school—sex, guns, drugs, gangs, bullying. Perhaps it's no wonder our kids don't seem to be getting the education they need to compete in a global economy. And it is also why private schools are booming.

One thing that is changing education today, and is maybe swinging the pendulum back to home education, is the Internet and the increasing number of children being homeschooled. I have friends who homeschool their kids, and their kids' test scores are very high in comparison to students at the public school. Another friend has a boy who is gifted in tennis. He attends a full-time tennis academy and takes classes on the Internet. Another friend has a daughter who is a talented actress. She lives in New York with her mother and also takes classes on the Internet. My own daughter and son-in-law are seriously considering homeschooling their twin boys next year.

In sum, it is not hard to see all the laws on our lenses that have changed over the years. Some changed for the better, but most did not, in my opinion. The long-term effects of a poorly educated nation will take time to measure, but I am fearful.

My father was the principal of a junior high school for his whole career. He devoted himself to the education of children. I remember him telling me about Elizabeth Duncan Koontz, the first black president of the National Education Association (NEA), who quoted a common Vietnam era phrase when she said, "I dream of the day when we have all the money we need for education in America and the Pentagon has to have a bake sale to buy a bomb." We need to fix our education system in America, but the fix is not more money from the federal government.

19

Visionaries and Others Who Change Our Lives

I know a story about a man who had a masonry business. He observed his workers carefully as they were laying bricks for a new church. Over time he noticed that one of his bricklayers had a much higher quality of work than the others. In addition, he was able to lay at least one-third more bricks than his fellow workers. The owner was curious and wanted to know why this one man was both faster and better than the other bricklayers. So he went to each of his men and asked them what they were doing? The answer consistently came back, "I'm laying bricks, sir." And certainly that was what each of them was doing. Then he came to his best and fastest bricklayer and he asked him, "What are *you* doing?" The man answered, "I'm building a cathedral, sir."

The difference for this one man was that he had a different law on his lens than the other bricklayers. The whole world occurred for him through a lens that said, "I'm building a cathedral." He wasn't laying bricks; he was doing something much more powerful, much more positive. His view had a purpose, and it enabled him to be better and faster. It is the old example of the glass half-full or half-empty. The laws on your lens shape how you think about everything. When you think you are building a cathedral, will that drive how you feel? Certainly. It is inspiring to be building a cathedral.

Is the way he felt affecting his actions? Of course. He's better and faster. Is that going to meet his needs over time? You know it will.

NASA

There are examples of this principle in all our lives. NASA was established in 1958. It employed thousands of people, including scientists, mathematicians, engineers, carpenters, propulsion specialists, and chemical engineers. They were all very busy doing their thing, making their contribution to the cause.

One day in 1961, President John F. Kennedy said, "We're going to put a man on the moon by the end of the decade." And that changed everything! Suddenly the people at NASA weren't doing science and math and engineering anymore. They were *putting a man on the moon*! Do you think that changed the way they thought about their jobs? Do you believe that change in thinking changed what they did? It obviously did, because Neil Armstrong walked on the moon in 1969, before the end of the decade.

When Kennedy said we were going to the moon, he had no idea what science would be required. He had no idea what it was going to cost. He had no idea how many people it would take or if it was even possible. But he changed the way everybody thought about space exploration. And with that one simple little law change, the lenses of NASA and the American people were changed forever.

Olympics

I experienced a similar phenomenon on a smaller scale in 1990. At that time, the Organizing Committee for the Olympic Games was looking for a host city for the 1996 Summer Olympics. A man in Atlanta, Georgia, named Billy Payne said, "I'm going to bring the 1996 Summer Olympic Games to Atlanta." He and Andrew Young and Atlanta Mayor Maynard Jackson set about to make that happen. They assembled a team of people and assigned tasks to thousands of volunteers. Hundreds of new jobs were created, and every person had one thing in common—they all were bringing the Olympics to Atlanta. It changed the way all of us thought. It changed what we felt and what we did. And when we won the bid, it changed the way every Atlantan thought.

September 11

If you're not old enough to remember Kennedy or the 1996 Summer Olympics, you should be old enough to remember September 11, 2001. Everybody remembers where they were when those planes flew into the towers of the World Trade Center. Other than the Revolutionary War against the British, no foreign enemy has ever fought on our land. While Pearl Harbor in Hawaii is technically the United States, Hawaii wasn't a state in 1941 and it isn't part of the continental United States. Up until 9/11, I believe that all of us had a law on our lenses that said, "We are safe from foreign attack." Not anymore.

That day changed national security. It created a department called Homeland Security. It created the Patriot Act. It created enhanced interrogation techniques. It changed the process and procedure for boarding airplanes. It changed the way some Americans viewed Muslims. And it changed the way most of us think about terrorism and how we took our safety for granted. In short, it changed how we think. As proof, do you still think the same about people wearing turbans or hijabs who are getting on an airplane with you? Probably not, if you're honest about it. Did it change what you do? Ask any TSA person if he or she unconsciously profiles people who fit terrorist characteristics. They do, and you want them to. The results so far seem to meeting our needs since we've not had another 9/11. But you should not get complacent. With Osama bin Laden's death in May 2011, we all need to remain on alert for any and all terrorist threats.

One of the planes involved on 9/11 was United Flight 93, which took off from Newark and crashed in a field in Pennsylvania. There have been movies made and books written about the heroics of the passengers on that flight. Experts believe the plane was headed for either the White House or the Capitol. While I have never doubted the heroics of those on board, I have often wondered how that plane actually came down after communication was lost.

President Bush had ordered the FAA to ground all planes. Military fighters were launched with the authority to shoot down any plane that did not comply. Is it possible that Flight 93 was shot down by one of our own fighters? While we'll never know for sure, it is probably unlikely.

But what if a fighter pilot in a similar situation was ordered to shoot down a passenger plane filled with his own countrymen and women? I'm sure the pilot would follow orders. Afterward though, would he be left with the thought that he had just killed hundreds of his own people, or that he had just saved the president of the United States? One of those two thoughts would be indelibly etched in his mind. It would become a law on his lens that would forever shape the way the world occurred for him. Imagine the difference between these two laws and how they would affect the way he felt and the way he behaved. The difference between those two laws would create drastically different results. And one would probably meet his needs over time, whereas the other would not. The power of the mind controls everything.

Mr. Curry

When I was in high school, I had a black physical education teacher named Rupert Curry. He also coached football and baseball. I played football, basketball, and baseball in high school, so I got a large dose of Mr. Curry. He was a big man, very outgoing, very confident, and very intimidating to high schoolers. But he was one of the most likeable people I'd ever met. Our relationship matured into friendship as well as teacher/student and coach/player.

I had never been around black people before, and as a ninth-grader I was curious. I think it is safe to say that my grandparents taught me prejudice. My parents, on the other hand (the first to go to college in either of their families), just ignored racial issues. So if I had any inclination prior to meeting Rupert Curry, I would have to say I was a skeptic about black people.

During my four years of high school, where I saw Mr. Curry every day, he treated me fairly, and I came to learn that Rupert Curry was just a good man, not a good black man. After I graduated, Mr. Curry left teaching and became a recruiter for IBM. Later he hired me as a computer programmer, and I worked for IBM for several years. During that time Rupert (which is what I called him by then) and I coached Little League football together, and our friendship grew. I was now married with children, and our families did many things together. I think his children thought I was part of the family.

The point I'm making is that once I looked beyond the color of Rupert's skin, I came to realize that he put his pants on one leg at a time just like me. When his family said grace before meals, he prayed to the same God I did. He treated me like I was one of his own children. The only difference between us was the color of our skin. I like to say that if I was a bigot before meeting Rupert Curry, he just loved the prejudice right out of me. All the laws on my lens regarding judging people were forever changed, and Rupert Curry put those new laws there. Those new laws meet my needs, and I will be forever grateful to him.

Rupert died several years ago. His family invited me to speak at his funeral, which I was glad to do. Among other things, I quoted a poem that Rupert taught all his football players.

> Dear Lord, as we go through the battle of life,
> We ask for a field that is fair.
> A chance that is equal for those in strife,
> A chance to do and to dare.
> And if we should win, let it be by our code,
> With our faith and our honor held high.
> But if we should lose, let us stand by the road,
> And cheer as the winners go by.

I learned that poem forty-eight years ago and can still quote it from memory to this day. Other than my mother and father, nobody influenced my life more than Rupert Curry.

Gunnar

When our oldest son and his wife were expecting their first child, we were all very excited and eager for the big day. She was about thirty-four weeks pregnant when suddenly she didn't feel right and the baby didn't seem to be moving. She went to the doctor right away. The news was bad. The heart had stopped beating. The baby was dead. The umbilical cord had gotten wrapped around him. She delivered a dead baby.

The baby had a name. We had all been calling him Gunnar for months. His loss was devastating. Not only were Sherrie and I grieving over the loss of a grandson, we had to watch our children in agony. One of the hardest things we did was bringing them home empty-handed. The nursery was ready. The shower gifts were all there. The crib. The toys. Everything but the baby. It was one of the most difficult things I have ever done in my life. There is nothing you can say. So we hugged them and helped them cry.

In that tragedy, there was a silver lining—our son and daughter-in-law grew so much closer together. It better prepared them for the parenthood that was soon to come. Their love for each other grew enormously as they leaned on each other for comfort and understanding. And I believe that the experience with Gunnar played a large part in their spiritual journey as well.

Since then they have had two beautiful girls. The oldest one is about to graduate from high school and go on to college. Through their experience with Gunnar, the laws on my son's and daughter-in-law's lenses about love, about being a good spouse, and about being a good parent had all changed. The girls were the beneficiaries. We celebrate Gunnar's birthday every year, and we're thankful for how he changed our lives. We certainly don't take the joy of grandchildren for granted anymore.

20

Do the Right Thing and
Do It Right Now

Some of the most significant shifts in America in my lifetime have been to our morals and values. I don't even know where to begin. There are just so many aspects to those terms: morals and values. Each person probably has a list of the component pieces as they define those words, and naturally I have mine. In this chapter we will explore fifteen attributes of morals and values. We will examine the differences in the laws on our lenses concerning these attributes between today and two hundred years ago. Also, we will try to compare our thoughts today as opposed to what our forefathers thought when founding our country.

Capital Punishment

There are two prevalent laws on the lenses of Americans today. First is the law that says, "Life is sacred, we should never take a life." This law seems to be upheld by many conservatives, and they hold this view for both criminals and the unborn. Second is the law that says, "In certain cases, taking another life is okay." This law seems to be found on the lenses of many liberals, and applies to criminals, pregnant women, self-defense, and war. I am not saying one is right and the other is wrong. But whichever law you have on your lens, that law will drive what you think and do, which will in turn create very different results.

One thing America has never come to grips with is whether prisons are there to punish inmates or rehabilitate them. Again, whichever side you take on this debate, that law that will drive your thinking and behavior. Years ago prisons believed in hard labor. Today, many jails are like country clubs, with TVs, recreation facilities, and more. The laws on our lenses today about what prison should be like are very different from one hundred years ago. Are they better or worse?

Today more than two million people are incarcerated in the United States—about one out of every 150 people. Another five or six million people are on probation or parole. Even worse is that 20 percent of inmates are considered mentally ill. Almost 80 percent of released inmates return to prison, which doesn't speak well of our rehabilitation efforts.[32]

I wonder whether our forefathers ever envisioned an America where one in every 150 people was in prison. I don't think so. Somewhere along the way we changed some laws on our lenses that led to our current condition, and from my perspective it is certainly not meeting my needs.

Violent Crime

One of the biggest reasons our prisons are so full is that there is so much crime. There seem to be many reasons for this increase. The biggest cause is probably the prevalence of drugs in our society. Another one is the large increase in impoverished illegal immigrants. More recently, unemployment and foreclosures have probably led some to pursue illegal activities.

Following are some statistics about crime and prisons in America:[33]

- America has an incarceration rate of 743 per 100,000, the highest of any country in the world.
- Twenty-five percent of all the world's prisoners are housed in the United States.

- The United States houses more prisoners than the top thirty-five European counties *combined.*
- The federal prison population has more than doubled since 1995.
- On average, former inmates' annual incomes are 40 percent less than those who have never been in prison.
- One in every twenty-eight children has an incarcerated parent. (Twenty-five years ago that ratio was one in every 125 children.)
- More than one in three young black men without a high school diploma is in prison. Of all black men without a high school diploma, more are incarcerated than employed.
- In the last fifty years, the population in America has doubled while the crime rate has tripled.

Do you think our Founding Fathers could have imagined such statistics? What happened to us? I believe that subtly, over time, some people have replaced laws on their lenses that say, "You should not steal" with "I want it, so I'm taking it." And we've watched on the sideline and done nothing. Know why? Because we've changed a law on our lenses from, "We won't let them get away with it" to, "I don't want to get involved. Besides, the problem is too big for *me* to fix, or it's not really affecting *my* life day to day."

The results we're producing are not meeting our needs. This suggests that we have some bad laws on our lenses, and for the sake of our grandchildren we need to change them.

Infidelity

A 2008 survey by *USA Today* found that more than half (54 percent) of Americans know someone who has been unfaithful to his or her spouse.[34] That is more than double the rate since 1964, when the percentage was just 24 percent. This would indicate that there has been a change of law on the lenses of most Americans. The law that said, "I believe in the sanctity of marriage and in faithfulness to my spouse," has given way to the law that says, "Saying

'I do' didn't mean exclusivity." Who knows what caused such a change in thinking? Perhaps there are many factors, like pornography, the Internet, more publicity about affairs. Just look at few of the statistics in the United States:[35]

- The percentage of marriages where either or both spouses admit to infidelity is 41 percent.
- The percentage of all marriages that end in divorce is 53 percent.
- The infidelity rate for men is 57 percent; for women it is 54 percent.
- The average length of an affair is two years.

But the most alarming statistic is how many people would cheat on their spouse if they knew they wouldn't get caught—74 percent of men and 68 percent of women.

What is this saying to our children? How did we degenerate as a nation so quickly? How come nobody is doing anything about this epidemic? My own personal belief is that the law on the lenses of most Americans that used to say, "Morals and values are essential to our character and our personal integrity," unfortunately now says, "I just don't care."

Divorce

With the infidelity rate so high, and most Americans apparently complacent about that, is it any wonder that our divorce rate is over 50 percent? And the statistics don't get better with practice. For second marriages, the divorce rate jumps to 67 percent; for third marriages, an astounding 73 percent.[36] The more we try, the worse we get, it would seem.

Another factor that makes the divorce rate even more startling is that so many people today opt to live together rather than get married. In 2007, 6.4 million opposite-sex couples were living together. That was an increase of 28 percent from the previous year, and an eightfold increase since 1978, when there were fewer than one million couples living together.[37] You can reasonably assume that these numbers have increased since 2007. The reason might be the financial stress created by unemployment, foreclosures, and the economic downturn.

It appears to me that the law that said, "Marriage is forever" has been replaced with, "If it doesn't work out, we'll just get divorced." People simply run off to Vegas or Mexico or some other place and get a quick divorce, or sometimes even an annulment.

Before you get married, you need to know your intended's past. He or she might promise that things will change once you're married, but past behavior trumps promises every time. If your intended has a drug problem, a pornography problem, or a debt problem, he or she is going to bring that problem into the marriage, and the problem won't get better just because you're married. My pastor says that there are no marriage problems, only people with problems who bring their problems into the marriage.

It seems that the law that said, "Marriage is the way" now says, "Living together first is better." However, studies show that the divorce rate for couples who live together first is no better than those couples who don't. In fact, some studies show that what is developing is *serial cohabitation,* as people move from cohabitant to cohabitant. The most significant law that has changed is that cohabitation is now acceptable, and worse, nobody cares that it has become acceptable. There seems to be a crisis in confidence about the institution of marriage.

Drugs

When I was in high school in the early 1960s, I can honestly say that I never even heard of illegal drugs, let alone knew anyone who was using them. But by the late '60s, college campuses were rife with illegal drug use. Certainly the rock music of the day played its part in the proliferation of drugs, as groups like the Beatles, the Rolling Stones, the Doors, and others sang about drugs all the time.

I guess every generation has its thing, and my generation's was beer. And I suppose if I had been born twenty years later and the bad-boy temptation was pot instead of beer, I would have participated. But I think the law on our lenses that changed between these two generations is that in my day the law said, "Be careful and don't hurt yourself." Today it seems to say, "If it makes you feel good it's okay, even if it's harmful."

Everyone seems to be looking for a high, even though the consequences are much more serious than in my day. In my mind anyway, marijuana, cocaine, methamphetamines, and heroin are all inherently more dangerous than beer. Illegal drug use in America today seems to be at epidemic proportions.

Consider the following:[38]

- America has the highest level of illegal drug use in the world.
- Americans are four times more likely to use cocaine in their lifetime than citizens of the country with the second-highest proportion of drug use.
- Forty-two percent of Americans admit to having smoked pot.
- Fifteen percent of Americans over twelve years of age have used an illegal drug within the last year.
- In the age group eighteen to twenty-five, that percentage jumps to 35 percent.
- Fifteen percent of all arrests in the United States are for drug violations, and 4 percent of all homicides are drug related.
- Twenty percent of state prisoners and 53 percent of federal prisoners are incarcerated for drug violations.
- Almost 40 percent of people on parole or probation have committed a drug offense.

The sale and use of drugs affects almost every aspect of our lives. The annual economic cost alone is estimated at $215 billion. Drug use and addiction overburden the judicial system, strain the health care system, reduce productivity, help destroy the environment, and damage countless families.

The impact is not limited to the drug user. One in ten children under eighteen lives with an addicted or drug-abusing parent. Substance abuse is a factor in nearly 70 percent of all foster care placements. When parents use methamphetamine, children are not only exposed to abuse and neglect, but fires, explosions, and toxic chemicals.

So how have we degenerated so far in the last forty years? If drug use was a medical condition affecting this number of people, we would have demanded a solution. Why do we let this continue? The law on our lenses now seems to say, "If it doesn't affect me directly, I really don't care. Let someone else worry about it." We no longer take a stand for the common good.

Fatherlessness

I touched briefly on fatherlessness earlier, but now I want to review it in more depth. Fatherlessness is a *tremendous* problem in America. Fatherlessness is approaching parity with fatherhood as a defining feature of American childhood. Whereas the law on our lenses used to say, "I am responsible for the lives I bring into the world," it now says, "Let the mother take care of the children," or sometimes, "Let the government take care of them." Never before in the history of America have so many children been voluntarily abandoned by their fathers.

I believe that fatherlessness is one of the most harmful demographic trends of our generation. It is the engine driving many of our social problems, like crime, teenage pregnancy, violence against women, and child abuse. The worst thing, however, is the apparent prevailing thought that not much can be done about it. We address all our other problems, like unemployment, economic downturn, foreclosures, gun control, and wars. But when it comes to men abdicating their responsibilities as fathers, nothing gets done. We avoid discussing the correlation between our social problems and fatherlessness.

The basic law that seems to have changed is the one that said, "A child needs a father." Its replacement seems to be, "Fathers are not necessary for rearing children." The worst part is that everyone seems to think that this change is okay. What is at stake is nothing less than what it means to be a man, who our children will become, and what kind of society we are evolving into.

Premarital Sex

The law on my lens growing up as a kid was, "Sex is forbidden outside of marriage." Sex was intended to bond a man and woman together and for procreation. Somehow we have evolved to a law that says, "Sex is for fun and intended for everyone, regardless of age or gender." Most people today think it is a waste of time to teach abstinence, and that we should just teach people about protection from pregnancy and disease. Today it is estimated that 75 percent of Americans have had premarital sex by age twenty.[39]

Television is a good example of how our thinking has changed over the last fifty years. Fifty years ago, Lucy and Ricky Ricardo slept in separate twin beds. Today we have shows like *Two and a Half Men* that celebrate premarital sex and infidelity.

What has been the effect of these changes? Well, there are approximately 4,000 abortions in America each day (over fifty million since 1973), and one-third of all girls in America gets pregnant before they are twenty—the highest rate in the industrialized world.[40]

Within fifty years we have gone from sexual repression to sexual obsession, made obvious by the current popularity of pornography. We have evolved to where the definition of a virgin is an ugly third-grader. In the 1960s, 75 percent of Americans believed premarital sex was wrong. By 1985 only 35 percent thought it was wrong. Today, my belief is that it has dropped to 25 percent.[40]

This sexual revolution, combined with the free-love sixties, drugs, and television, has created many detrimental effects: more children born out of wedlock, more fatherless children, children having sex at younger ages, more abortions, and more sexually transmitted diseases. And these problems seem to be getting worse.

Sex is more than a physical act, more than just a pleasurable activity. It is an act of body and soul that unites a man and a woman and allows them to create families. Outside this purpose, sex negatively impacts society. Where you find premarital sex to be prevalent, you will find broken homes, teenage pregnancies, abortions, and disease. How could we have gotten here? Why did we let these laws change?

Profanity

My mother would wash my mouth out with soap if she heard me use a swear word. But worse than that, she would also tell my father, who would wear my butt out with a belt. Today, however, profanity seems to be prevalent everywhere, particularly on television. The law on my lens as a kid was, "Profanity is wrong." Today it seems to be, "Profanity is just like any other word."

Seventy percent of Americans today report hearing profanity in public frequently. Two-thirds say that people swear more today than they did even twenty years ago. And surprisingly, 32 percent of men admit to using the F-word a few times per week, and 23 percent of women. [41]

I saw some statistics recently based on tape-recorded conversations. The findings showed that swear words were used on average 80–90 times per day—.5 percent to .7 percent of all words.[42]

My own experience is that people who frequently use swear words have a limited vocabulary. But why do we tolerate so much profanity? And why has it become so much more prevalent in the last fifty years? What is the impact of profanity on our children? Do we even care? If we do, how do we fix it?

Pornography

Do you think that Thomas Jefferson envisioned pornography as part of the First Amendment right to free speech? If not, then it is clear that this law on our lenses has certainly changed. Why have we allowed this to happen to our country?

Pornography today features sadomasochism, incest, bestiality, group sex, bisexuality, and necrophilia. This is a sick and violent business. And people are becoming addicted to it, particularly on the Internet. In 2005, it was estimated that 10 percent of American adults were sex addicts, and that 28 percent of those are women. Forty million US adults regularly visit Internet pornography websites.[43] Just look at some of these statistics to see what a widespread problem pornography has become:[43]

- The pornography industry's annual revenues exceed that of Microsoft, Google, Amazon, eBay, Yahoo, Apple, and Netflix *combined.*
- Worldwide revenues from pornography exceed $100 billion.
- There are over two million pornographic websites.
- More than 25,000 images of child porn are posted online every week.
- Twenty percent of all Internet porn involves children (over 150,000 websites).
- Nine out of ten children between the age of eight and sixteen have viewed porn on the Internet.
- The average age of someone's first porn exposure is eleven.

Among ministers, 57 percent say that pornography is the most damaging issue to their congregations. In American families, 47 percent say pornography is a problem in their home.[43] Internet porn is a significant factor in two-thirds of all divorces. This is having a huge impact on our country, especially on our children. Listen to these statistics about the impact of pornography on children:[43]

- One in ten children who use the Internet are sexually solicited.
- One in five children receive unwanted sexual solicitations online.
- Of children between the ages of fifteen and seventeen who are abducted, 40 percent are from Internet contact.

Pornography is addictive. Addicts get immersed in their fantasies and develop a sense that "everybody does it." Their addiction rules their lives. We are raising children who are being exposed to pornography, which will alter their futures. Experts estimate that as many as one in three girls and one in seven boys will be sexually molested before they are eighteen. Staggering!

Dr. Jennings Bryant recently said, "If the values which permeate the content of hardcore pornography continue, we can forget trust, forget family, forget love, and forget marriage. In this world of ultimate physical hedonism, anything goes."[43] And the Justice Department was recently quoted as saying, "Never before in the history of telecommunications media in the United States has so much indecent and obscene material been so easily accessible to so many minors, in so many American homes, with so few restrictions."

I wonder how Mr. Thomas Jefferson would describe the change in our thinking today. How could the laws on our lenses have changed so dramatically in just over two hundred years? How and why did we let this happen? If we continue to ignore the seriousness of pornography, we are consciously contributing to the corruption of our society and our children. And if God does not somehow punish the United States of America for allowing this moral decline, then I believe He owes Sodom and Gomorra an apology.

Abortion

When our Founding Fathers crafted the Constitution and its later amendments, there was no specific language regarding abortion. I believe its absence is because they never considered it possible that the value of human life would ever be reduced to so little. Whereas the law on the lenses of our Founding Fathers was, "Sanctity of life," many Americans' lenses now say, "Pregnant women have the right to terminate their pregnancies."

It used to be that states had abortion laws. But in 1973 a Supreme Court decision (by a vote of seven to two) in Roe vs. Wade, deemed abortion to be a fundamental right under the Constitution. This decision prompted a national debate that continues to this day. It created issues about whether, and to what extent, abortion should be legal. It created questions about who should decide the legality of abortion, what methods the Supreme Court should use in Constitutional adjudication, and what the role of religious groups should be. Roe vs. Wade reshaped national politics, dividing most of the nation into pro-life and pro-choice groups while activating grassroots movements on both sides.

Today there are about 1.2 million abortions each year. Since the 1973 Roe vs. Wade decision, over fifty million pregnancies have been terminated.[44] This is more deaths in fifty years than the population of many countries, and approximately equal to the number of lives lost in World War II.

I'm not even sure how you measure the impact of this phenomenon on our society. We just don't value life like our Founding Fathers did. In fact, we're even schizophrenic about it. Why are abortions legal and euthanasia is not? Dr. Kevorkian (who died in 2011), who was often referred to as the doctor of death, was just trying to help people leave life with dignity. Abortions prevent life from occurring *without* the consent of the life in question. How can one be legal and the other not? Either all life is sacred, or no life is sacred.

I am an all-life-is-sacred guy. I believe George Washington and John Adams thought so too. So how did this law on our lens get so distorted? Do you think that the results of this change are meeting our country's needs?

Tolerance and Absolutes

The Founding Fathers of this country believed in absolutes. It was a law on their lenses. They believed in God, they believed it was wrong to kill, and they believed it was wrong to steal. These were absolute truths to them. They believed in physical truths like the law of gravity, the law of force equals mass times acceleration, and 2 + 2 = 4. They believed in the existence of absolute moral and spiritual doctrines. These included the existence of axiomatic principles or values that are timeless, unchanging, complete, not doubted, unencumbered, unconditional, self-evident, and *not relative.*

Today, however, we live in a world of relativism, with no absolutes. Our mantra is a tolerance of everything, with a proclivity for situational ethics. The only absolute of today is *no absolutes.* Today, everything is relative. Relativists deny the existence of moral and spiritual absolutes and declare that all values are relative, differing according to circumstances, situations, persons, cultures, conditions, and any other variable that suits their needs. While declaring that there are no absolute truths, relativists promote their own brand of truth. Their only acknowledged constant is change.

We have to be tolerant of the Muslim faith and allow them to bow toward Mecca, but Christians can't pray in school. We have to be tolerant of immigrants, minorities, gays, socialists, and the KKK. The ACLU takes up all these causes of tolerance. Where does it stop? Will we soon have to be tolerant of rapists, thieves, anarchists, and murderers? It is a very slippery slope, and unfortunately we seem to be near the bottom.

Tolerance used to mean putting up with someone or something you didn't especially like. Today tolerance means, "All values, all beliefs, all lifestyles, and all truths are equal." Denying this new definition of tolerance makes you intolerant and worthy of contempt. The new definition makes Christian claims to exclusivity intolerant, which supposedly justifies all the anti-Christianity in the media.

I want relativists to be fair. If tolerance is the watchword, why can't they be tolerant of my absolutes? If everything can be done and tolerated in accordance with one's own opinion, what about my opinion? What about my absolutes? Relativists and absolutists are hypocrites.

How and why have we allowed the law of absolutes to be changed to relativism? It seems to me that the law of love is vastly superior to the law of tolerance:

- Tolerance avoids offending anyone; love promotes the good of another person. Tolerance says, "You must approve of what I do;" whereas love says, "I will love you even when your behavior offends me."
- Tolerance says, "You must agree with me." Love says, "I will tell you the truth, because the truth will set you free."
- Tolerance says, "You *must* allow me to have my way." Love says, "I will plead with you to follow the *right* way, because I believe you are worth it."
- Tolerance seeks to be inoffensive; love takes risks.
- Tolerance glorifies division; love seeks unity.
- Tolerance costs nothing; love costs everything.

Let us change the law on our lenses that says, "Be tolerant of one another," to "Love one another." I am certain that it will better meet our needs over time.

Integrity and Honesty

The core of any individual, institution, or nation is honesty and integrity. Webster's New World Dictionary defines integrity as "the quality or state of being of sound moral principle." I believe this to be true, and therefore honesty is really a part of integrity. Part of being morally sound is being honest. Do you think that Alexander Hamilton would look at America today and think that our country, our people, and our institutions have integrity? I think he would throw up at the lack of integrity at every level.

Moral decay has infiltrated our very core. Americans are increasingly convinced that their political leaders, government officials, and financial and business leaders have not been honest with America. We are to blame, for it starts with each of us as an individual. We need to be held accountable for allowing this lack of integrity to continue over the years. Each person in America must commit to personal integrity and demand it from others, if we are to bring about any change. The law on our lenses needs to be, "I will do nothing without total honesty and integrity."

If our presidents don't have integrity, how can we expect our country to have integrity? How do you think our Founding Fathers would view Richard Nixon's Watergate incident and cover-up or Bill Clinton's sexual escapades in the Oval Office? These men have no integrity. Social Security and Medicare are not sustainable, and Congress doesn't have enough integrity to tell the American people that and to fix it.

What about the leaders of Enron, Freddie Mac, and Fannie Mae, and a Congress that spends $14 trillion that we don't have? These people have no integrity either. And what about the individual who cheats on both his or her spouse and his or her taxes; the person who makes child pornography; the person who sells drugs to our kids; the fathers who abandon their children? These people have no integrity. There is a lack of integrity at every level.

The filmmaker Sam Goldwyn is alleged to have said, "The most important thing in acting is honesty. Once you've learned to fake that, you're in." Doesn't that fit our country today? To me integrity only requires three simple things: discerning what is right and what is wrong; acting on what you have discerned, even at personal cost; and saying openly that you are acting on your understanding of right and wrong. That's it!

Lying, Cheating, Stealing

You know the story of George Washington and the cherry tree. He told his father he could not tell a lie, so we can assume the law on his lens was,

"Lying is wrong." Today the law on our lenses says, "Lying is okay, if you don't get caught." We've come a long way since the time of Washington, and lying, cheating, and stealing are now prevalent in America. In a recent survey among high school students about lying, cheating, and stealing, the results show:[45]

- 28 percent stole something from a store in the last year.
- 23 percent stole something from a parent or relative.
- 19 percent stole something from a friend.
- 42 percent said they sometimes lie to save money.
- 60 percent cheated on a test during the past year.
- 36 percent used the Internet to plagiarize an assignment.
- 23 percent cheated to win a sporting event.
- 82 percent admitted to lying to their parents.
- 62 percent lie to teachers.

The real irony is that these same students reported to have a high regard for honesty, trust, and good character. There certainly seems to be a big gap between what we think and what we do.

One of the reasons our nation has plummeted to these lows is that so many people seem to have a new law on their lenses that says, "It must be okay, since everybody is doing it." The response to that kind of thinking is that nothing is "out there"; everything is "in here." You are only responsible for you. It makes no difference what everyone "out there" is doing. It only matters what you are doing.

Homosexuality

I'll bet that Thomas Jefferson never dreamed there would be a day in America when we would celebrate gay rights, and that nearly 40 percent or more of Americans would acknowledge homosexuality as a "normal variant within human sexuality."[46] There is no doubt that homosexuality existed in Jefferson's day, but it was viewed as abnormal, wrong, and sinful.

The American Psychological Association classified homosexuality as a mental disorder as recently as 1952. After that, the notion of homosexuality as a mental disorder began to erode. In 1973, the association reversed its position and encouraged psychiatrists to "take the lead in removing the stigma of mental illness that had long been associated with homosexual orientations."

Perhaps homosexuality is not a mental illness. But many today believe it is a *normal* variant in sexual orientation. I bet none of the men who signed the Declaration of Independence thought homosexuality was a normal variant. Clearly something on our lenses has changed. The law that said, "Homosexuality is wrong, abnormal, and immoral," has been replaced by many with a law that says, "Homosexuality is a normal variant of a person's sexuality."

In an exit poll on election day in 2008, approximately 5 percent of the people identified themselves as gay, lesbian, or bisexual. That would be approximately fifteen to eighteen million people. That is a lot of people. But numbers don't make it right from my perspective.

Personally, I believe that homosexuality is wrong and socially destructive. I am convinced that the Bible is clear on the subject, and that an empirical analysis of homosexuality will corroborate the biblical assessment that homosexuality is not what God intends for individuals or society. This same opinion was held by our Founding Fathers. But today homosexuality is being forced on us through legislation, taught to our children in schools, and promoted by the arts and entertainment industry. Remember, you must be tolerant. Our founders are rolling over in their graves.

Centrality of God

God was central to the belief system of our Founding Fathers. We began as a Christian nation, and the men who fought for our independence were prayer warriors who called on God with great regularity and faithfulness.

Since that time we put the words "under God" in our Pledge of Allegiance. We put "in God we trust" on all our money. If God was not central to the lives of the Founding Fathers and those who came after them, then why would they have done this?

Somewhere along the way we have lost our roots, the fundamental beliefs that started this great nation. I believe that every subject in this chapter, all of which represent a steep moral decline, can be traced back to our diminished view of God as the central theme to our lives and to our country.

In the early 1960s, the United States Supreme Court banned prayer and Bible reading in public schools. The woman most commonly associated with these rulings is Madalyn Murray O'Hair. She was an atheist who brought a lawsuit against her school district because she didn't want her son exposed to Christianity. Incredibly, the Supreme Court ruled eight to one that prayer and Bible reading in school was unconstitutional. Do you think for one minute that this is what our Founding Fathers intended when they wrote the Constitution?

We seem to have separated God from our country. Many have laid siege upon Christianity, seeking to excise all Christian influence from American government and its institutions. It has been done piecemeal, like banning prayer in schools, banning the Ten Commandments from our courthouses, and allowing government-funded abortions. These same people are convinced that God has no place in American governance. They steadfastly cling to the false belief that the First Amendment implies mandatory separation.

For years, what was considered American was also considered Christian. The two terms were almost synonymous. To be Christian was to be American, and to be an American was to be Christian. The value system of America was the value system of Christianity. It is what made our nation great. Separating the two is causing our downfall. You can't replace faith in God with faith in government or faith in people. Communism didn't fail because socialism is evil; it failed because it excised God from the people's ideology.

The law on the lenses of our Founding Fathers was, "Almighty God is central to everything we do both as government and as individuals." Today we have laws on our lenses that make many different things our god, and therefore central to our lives. To some, their god is government, to some it is their job or their family, to some it is money, and to others it is power. What is your god? What has replaced Almighty God in your life? If you want your nation to regain the moral ground that it has lost over the last two hundred years, then you must start putting God back in the place where our forefathers intended Him to be. Absent this, all other work is futile.

21

Money Isn't Everything,
but It's Way up There

Everyone needs a financial plan and no age is too early to start. The habit of saving for a rainy day should begin early. My parents grew up during the Great Depression of the 1930s. The stock market had crashed, banks were closing, and many people lost everything they had. At this time, my grandfather worked for the Pennsylvania Railroad for five dollars per week. He and my grandmother raised five children on that income. They learned to pinch pennies, and they never spent money on anything they could do or make themselves.

Consequently, my dad grew up with a law on his lens that said, "Be thrifty in everything. Save everything you can." For all of his life, that law served him well.

Today, however, the laws of being thrifty and saving for the future seem to have changed to "I want instant gratification" and "I can spend everything I make." We live in a world of credit, where we borrow what we need to instantly gratify our desires. Even our Congress has this law, running up a $14 trillion debt with a law that says, "Deficit spending is okay."

Today many young families are dependent on two incomes to meet their budgetary needs. Kids are in after-school programs so Mommy can work. Few are saving for the future because their lifestyle today is more important than planning for their future needs. People have to have "that house, in that neighborhood," or "that car," or "that club membership." The law on the lenses of many people today seems to be, "I need it (or want it) now."

There are three laws that I would recommend for everyone to put on their lenses in regards to financial planning:

- Save 10 percent of everything you make—even that five dollars Grandma gives you every year for your birthday.
- Give 10 percent of everything you make to charity—beginning with that same five dollars.
- Never go into debt except for a house (and avoid even that if you can).

Everyone needs to plan for their financial future. You will have cars and houses to buy, children to rear, college to pay for, a retirement to fund. The time to start saving for those things is today. Then when the need arises, you will have the money you need. Plus, you will always be hit by unplanned emergencies that require money. It will be a great comfort to know that you have a financial cushion at those times.

The mathematics of compound interest should be taught in first grade. If you save ten dollars a week beginning at age ten, at 3 percent compound interest, you will have over $70,000 when you are sixty-five years old. Saving more each week is even better. If you invest your assets, you can earn even more, but there is risk in investing. The point is to get into a regular habit of saving. Start early and teach it to your kids. It will solve many future problems, and you'll sleep better too.

We all need to give back a portion of what we have. I have some friends who try to live on as little as possible so they can give more away. It is a tremendous feeling to know that you have helped someone else. You can give to charities, you can give to your church, you can give directly to people whom you know are in need. You can give in any number of ways.

In the book of Malachi, the last book of the Old Testament, God challenges His people to bring their tithe (that is, 10 percent) into the storehouse so that there will be food in the temple. God then says something unique. He says, "Test me in this matter, to see if I will not open for you the windows of heaven and pour out for you blessing until there is no room for it all." Now that is quite a challenge.

I decided to test the Lord as He suggested. I started giving 10 percent of everything I made to Him even when bills went unpaid. Today my house is paid for, my cars are paid for, I have no credit card debt, and no other debt of any kind. And I have enough money saved to last me the rest of my life. If you haven't done this already, test God for yourself and see what happens.

It is very tempting to go into debt. I know. I did it. I had house payments, car payments, furniture payments, and every other kind of payment you can imagine. If I could have it now and pay for it later, I did it. Eventually it caught up to me. I had to start getting rid of assets in order to pay my monthly bills. I learned too late. My recommendation for young people today is not to go into debt for anything other than a house. Generally a house appreciates (gains in value), whereas most everything else depreciates (loses value). Save until you have the cash to pay for something. Otherwise, don't get it. If you start saving when you're young, you should be in good shape. I know it is hard, but one day you'll thank me for that advice.

So in closing, please put these three laws on yours lenses: save 10 percent, give 10 percent to charity, and never go into debt for anything but a home. If the world can start occurring for you with these three laws on your lenses, then I believe the results you will create will best meet your needs over time.

22

What Will They Think of Next?

It is incredible to think of all the technological changes that have occurred in my lifetime. When I was born in 1947, television was brand new. Today we can get live, color, HD pictures from Mars. You might have seen not only the invention of the computer, but the advances to the point where today, almost everybody has one. Not to mention that your car probably has over twenty computers.

You've seen the proliferation of the Internet, with virtual access to anything and everything. You now have wireless technologies that allow anything to communicate with anything else without wires. You've seen men walk on the moon; you've seen people receive artificial hearts; you've seen laser-guided bombs; and you've seen global positioning systems that tell you where we are to within three feet. If my grandmother were alive today, she would not believe anything she saw. And if one of our Founding Fathers jumped forward in time, there are literally thousands of things he would see today that he would have trouble comprehending. Imagine explaining these to Thomas Jefferson:

- Hair dryers
- Toothpaste
- Automobiles
- Calculators

- Velcro
- Batteries
- Radio and TV
- Wristwatches
- Zippers
- Tupperware
- Aluminum foil
- Air-conditioning

This list could go on for quite a while. You have laws on your lens that say certain things just aren't possible. But technological change demands that you change that law to, "Anything is possible with technology."

Most of us look at change as linear, including technology. But conventional wisdom now thinks that technological change is exponential, not linear. That means that instead of things progressing like 1, 2, 3, 4, 5, they progress like 1, 4, 9, 16, 25.[47]

In his 1999 book *The Age of Spiritual Machines*, Ray Kurzweil proposed the Law of Accelerating Returns, which states that the rate of change in technology tends to increase exponentially. He gave further focus to this issue in a 2001 essay entitled "The Law of Accelerating Returns," in which he argues that whenever a technology approaches some kind of a barrier, new technology will be invented to allow us to cross that barrier.

He predicts that such paradigm shifts have and will continue to become increasingly common, leading to "technological change so rapid and profound it represents a rupture in the fabric of human history."

His analysis of the history of technology shows that we won't experience one hundred years of progress in the twenty-first century—but more like 20,000 years of progress (at today's rate).[47] He also believes that the speed of computer chips and their cost-effectiveness will increase exponentially. He says there will even be exponential growth in the rate of exponential growth. The implications for him include the merger of biological and non-biological intelligence, immortal software-based humans, and ultrahigh levels of intelligence that expand outward in the universe at the speed of light.

I think that what this all means is that you have no way of predicting what the next technology will be or what impact it will have on your life. I know that the law on my lens that said, "Change is slow" has been altered to say, "Change will come faster and faster." With that alteration, nothing new will ever surprise you and you will accept change more readily. It will give you the best chance to meet your needs over time.

23

They've Got a Cure for Everything

What used to be impossible in medicine is accepted today as ordinary. Like other technologies, medical technology seems to be changing exponentially. The laws on our lenses regarding medicine have changed from, "There is nothing you can do" to almost an expectation that, "Certainly there is a drug for that condition."

Since 1950, life expectancy has increased by a full decade.[48] People are living longer and healthier lives as a result of medical advances. There have been significant improvements in both the prevention and treatment of diseases and illnesses. In 1975, 49 percent of cancer patients were expected to live five years after detection. Today, 67 percent live five or more years after detection. Death from heart attack and heart failure fell by 50 percent between the years 2000 and 2005. Treatments for diabetes, rheumatoid arthritis, and osteoporosis have all seen dramatic improvements as a result of new medications.[49] In the last ten years alone, more than 300 new medicines have been brought to the market.[49] Where an HIV diagnosis was a death sentence thirty years ago, new drugs today offer great promise for extending life expectancy for those infected with this virus. New drugs are coming on the market to treat Alzheimer's disease. Medical technology is advancing so rapidly, I believe that within my lifetime we will see a cure, if not prevention, for both Alzheimer's disease and cancers of all kinds.

We now have not only neonatal care procedures, we also have procedures for treating and even operating on children still in the womb. Fifty years ago it was impossible to tell the sex of unborn children, and now you can operate on them. Imagine that. Once born, you have immunizations and inoculations for virtually every major disease or ailment, including meningitis, measles, diphtheria, hepatitis A and B, flu, mumps, whooping cough, polio, small pox, tetanus, chicken pox, and pneumonia.

There have also been significant advances in organ transplants and in artificial organs. Today it is possible to transplant hearts, kidneys, pancreases, livers, heart-lungs, and even limbs, like a hand. There are artificial hearts and pacemakers for heart rhythm problems. In years to come we will see continued breakthroughs in the area of transplants and artificial organs. And speaking of artificial, what about prosthetics? Today we have artificial arms, legs, and hands.

Surgical procedures have also seen tremendous change. Fifty years ago, removing a gall bladder would leave a scar that ran from your belly button to your backbone. Recovery was long and painful. Today, with laparoscopic technology, it is three small incisions and back to normal in a week. With arthroscopic surgery, athletes can have surgery on elbows, knees, ankles, and shoulders with the same three small incisions, and be back on the field in as little as two weeks. Endoscopic procedures allow doctors to tour patients' intestines to look for tumors, cancer, or blockages without intrusiveness.

There have also been enhancements in the world of radiology. Now we don't just have X-rays; we have magnetic resonance imaging, or MRIs. We also have CT scans, ultrasounds, and sonograms, all of which allow doctors to see problems more clearly, make better diagnoses, and prescribe better treatments.

And let's not forget plastic surgery. If you don't like your ears or nose, you can have them fixed to look however you want. Women flock to these doctors for nips and tucks to their lips, eyes, and chins. The whole cosmetic surgery business for breast enhancements, tummy tucks, face-lifts, eye-lifts, and you-name-it procedures, is a multibillion dollar industry.

Do you think for one minute that George and Tom (Washington and Jefferson, that is) ever conceived of the things that are possible today through medical technology and innovation? No way. In fact, most of it couldn't have been imagined by my grandmother fifty years ago. And the next fifty years will see an even greater rate of change.

The laws on your lens about what is possible through medical technology need to be changed every few months, because change is occurring that fast. Let me make an analogy between medicine and ATM machines. Years ago when ATMs first came into use, you always looked for a decal on the machine that matched the decal on your card. If it didn't match, you knew your card wouldn't work in that ATM. Today, most cardholders just assume that every card will work in every ATM and they don't even bother to look at the decal anymore. I believe this same phenomenon will happen in medicine. We are rapidly approaching a time when it will be our *expectation* that there is a cure, a pill, or a treatment for every medical condition. So the law on our lenses that said, "There is no cure" will shift to, "There either is or will be a cure." And if in the next fifty years our life expectancy increases by another decade, having enough money for retirement will likely be a bigger problem for us than our health care.

24

It's Not Nice to Fool Mother Nature

When I was in high school, ecology was a science class, only we called it earth science. There was no sense of endangering the environment, there was no awareness of greenhouse gases, and there was no concern about global warming. We had no idea that the carbon monoxide fumes from automobiles were having any significant impact on the environment.

At the same time, manufacturers were emitting smoke and gas into the air and dumping other waste into the water. I don't know if these companies had any idea about the harm they were doing. I certainly had no idea about the harm I was doing as an individual. Our culture has evolved today to where we have to deal with toxic waste and the radiation poisoning caused by nuclear energy.

The law on my lens when I was younger was, "Nothing I do really affects the environment." Now that law says, "Everything I do affects the environment."

The term ecology embraces six major components, as follows:[50]

- Biosphere—the earth's surface and the atmosphere
- Biomes—the earth's climates, like tropical rain forests and others
- Ecosystems—organisms and their interaction with their environment

- Communities
- Populations
- Organisms—living things

All of these components make up our ecology, and all are equally important.

In 1970, the Environmental Protection Agency (EPA) was formed to regulate any practice that might have an adverse effect on the environment. The EPA was the government's answer to industries and their unsafe practices that posed hazards to human health and the environment in general. Without the EPA's oversight for the last forty years, there is no telling how bad things would be today.

Since its inception, the EPA has monitored air, water, land, and human health. The EPA also researches ways to protect the environment, and is empowered to enforce regulations under environmental law. It is responsible for the Federal Water Pollution Control Act, the Safe Drinking Water Act, the Clean Air Act, the Federal Environmental Pesticide Control Act, and many other federal environmental statutes.

In 1996, along with the Department of Energy (DOE), the EPA promoted the reduction of energy consumption and greenhouse-gas emissions from power plants. Their efforts saved 180 billion kilowatt hours in 2007 alone, or the equivalent of approximately 5 percent of the total electricity demand in the United States.[51]

Now I am not necessarily a believer in global warming or in the eminent threat of greenhouse-gas emissions, but I do believe that we need to stop polluting our air and our water. We need to be more aware of the lives of plants and animals and be more considerate of their needs. Some species will become extinct if we don't.

You need to remain cognizant of things like acid rain, climate change, water and air quality, mold, lead, asbestos, radon, waste, recycling, and ultraviolet indexes. We certainly do not need another Exxon/Valdez oil spill in Alaska; or the more recent BP oil spill in the Gulf of Mexico. As we move forward with exponential change in almost everything, we need to be conscious of the needs of Mother Earth and not treat her with abuse or as an infinite resource. We need a law on our lenses that says, "Our ecology must be a consideration in everything we do."

25

Earth, Wind, and Sun—
More Power to You

One of the big concerns of our day is energy—its sources, types, availability, and impact. The automobile is largely powered by oil, a fossil fuel with significant impact on the environment. Most of the oil consumed in the United States is imported from foreign countries. I imagine most Americans would like to reduce their dependence on foreign oil. While natural gas and even hydrogen are making some advances, the automobile seems to be dependent on foreign oil for the foreseeable future.

Another major energy source in the United States is coal. Coal is used mostly today to generate electricity. One of the nice things about coal is that the United States possesses an abundance of it, and we're not dependent on other countries for this natural resource.

The law on my lens about energy used to be, "We'll always have plenty of it, there is no need to conserve it, and we won't need to buy it from other countries." And years ago I never had any fear of energy, but that changed with the advent of nuclear energy. The laws on my lenses are very different today.

To date, there have been four major nuclear disasters. The first was in 1945, when the United States dropped two atomic bombs on Japan.

Since then there has been Three Mile Island in the United States in 1979, in which a reactor was damaged but all radiation was contained and there were no major consequences. Then in 1986 at Chernobyl in Ukraine, a reactor was destroyed by a steam explosion and thirty-one people were killed. There were also significant health and environmental consequences.

And most recently, in 2011, at the Fukushima plant in Japan, four nuclear reactors were destroyed by an earthquake and the resulting tsunami, when the plant lost its ability to cool its reactors. The impacts on life, health, and the environment remain unknown. These accidents, regardless of their cause, are frightening, and a major disaster with catastrophic results could happen at any time.

As a result of the Fukushima disaster, Germany shut down seven reactors and its plans to extend reactor life beyond 2020 may be scrapped. Italy renewed its moratorium on nuclear power, and other European Union countries are reviewing their nuclear plans. Even here in the United States, new safety evaluations are underway to operate safely during earthquakes, terror attacks, flooding, and loss of power. According to Nathan Hultman, a climate policy expert, "The events at Fukushima will complicate planning for nuclear expansion for the coming years in all countries. Fukushima exposed what has always, and will always, persist with nuclear power—it is a technology that is perceived as dangerous and no amount of redundancy will ever be able to completely scrub the specter of nuclear risk from discussions of energy policy."[52]

What laws exist on your lens about nuclear energy? If your law says nuclear power is dangerous, what would you think about a nuclear power plant being built less than a mile from where you live? You would probably feel fear or perhaps even anger. If you feel fear, then what are you likely to do? You are probably going to do everything you can to stop it, or you are going to move, or you'll do both. The law on your lens drives what you feel, and your feelings drive what you do every time!

While nuclear reactors for power plants do not present any opportunity for explosion like a nuclear bomb, there is the constant fear of the uncontrolled release of radioactive material and its subsequent effect on human life and the environment. I remain fearful of nuclear energy, and I have a law on my lens that says, "Don't live next to a nuclear power plant."

Renewable Energy Sources

Several promising new renewable energy sources are now in use—solar, wind, and geothermal. Solar panels seem to be going up everywhere. My brother just installed them on his roof. Solar power is infinite and renewable. Researchers are now working on ways to incorporate solar power into the electrical grid.

Wind is basically a form of solar energy. Wind power is the process by which wind is used to generate mechanical or electrical power. Wind turbines convert the kinetic energy in the wind for mechanical purposes, like grinding corn or pumping water. A generator can also turn this mechanical power into electricity that can power homes, businesses, and schools. The stronger the wind blows the more power that gets generated. Wind energy is abundant in America. Areas known to have consistently high winds, like Chicago (the Windy City), represent a rich environment for wind-energy generation.

The most exciting new potential energy source for me is geothermal energy. Essentially, it is heat from the earth and it can be found anywhere, including your own backyard. Many regions of the world are already using geothermal energy. El Salvador, Iceland, and the Philippines generate more than 25 percent of their national electricity from geothermal plants. Twenty-four other countries already have geothermal plants producing over 9,000 megawatts. That's enough electricity to run twelve million American households for one year.[52]

The United States has more geothermal capacity than any other country in the world. California alone has forty geothermal plants, which supply 5 percent of the state's electricity.[53] Thousands of buildings and homes across the United States use geothermal heat pumps to both heat and cool. Below the earth's crust is a layer of molten rock called magma. The amount of heat within 10,000 meters of the earth's surface contains 50,000 times more energy than all the oil and gas resources in the world![53] The future of geothermal energy is incredibly bright. Incredible stuff!

One final renewable energy source is water. If we can economically separate the hydrogen from the oxygen in good old H_2O, then we can burn hydrogen. It could power our cars and heat our homes. A few prototype hydrogen cars already exist.

The laws on my lens regarding energy have changed. Whereas I used to think that fossil fuels like oil and coal were okay, I now think that those fuels offer only a limited supply, and they are more harmful to human life and our environment than the emerging alternatives. And while nuclear energy seems cost-effective with a long life cycle, it just scares me to death. Some natural disaster, if not a terrorist, will cause a meltdown and create an even bigger nuclear disaster. My money is on solar, wind, and geothermal energy. They are renewable, limitless, and friendly to both human life and the environment. We just need more research to make all them more cost-effective. And hopefully, that will happen soon.

26

She's a Lot More Than Just Pretty

The role of women in America has changed significantly in the last one hundred years. It wasn't until 1920 that women even gained the right to vote. Remember the expression "man of the house"? Well, those days seem long gone, and justifiably so.

The Glass Ceiling

Today, there are some well-known women who have finally broken through the glass ceiling–Carly Fiorina and Hillary Clinton, just to name two. But the majority of women still are not in the executive suite. According to the United States Census Bureau in 2005, the average female salary in America was about 75 percent that of her male counterpart.[54] And male executives seem to give preference to males at promotion time. Margery Elfin, co-author of the book *The Cost of Being Female*, says, "In twenty years, women will have come only four cents closer to being paid the same as men."[55]

Education

It wasn't too long ago that many people had a law on their lenses that said, "A woman's place is in the home." As a result, many women were not expected to go to college, but rather to stay at home and take care of their families. In Middle Eastern and North African countries, most women receive only an eighth-grade education, if that. In Afghanistan, only 18 percent of women between ages fifteen and twenty-four can read.[56] Even in the United States there are still schools today, like the Citadel and the Virginia Military Institute, that don't appear to give women an equal opportunity.

Military

Remember when the law on our lenses said, "Women can't do that." Well boy, has that changed. Women are now serving just about everywhere. Women are in combat situations, where previously that was prohibited. Women are piloting those F-16s that you see being launched off aircraft carriers, and they're carrying assault rifles in advanced positions on the battlefield.

Government

Of the five hundred thirty-five members of the United States Congress, ninety-four are women, just 17 percent.[57] In addition, of the fifty governors in the United States, only six are women.[58] While many today would argue that this is still too low a percentage, you have to consider that less than one hundred years ago, women couldn't even vote.

There have been some great women in political history. My personal favorite is Margaret Thatcher from Britain. I once heard her described as Ronald Reagan with balls. Condoleezza Rice stands out for me in the Bush administration, and Hillary Clinton in the Obama cabinet. I must say that I also really like Jan Brewer, the governor of Arizona. She is struggling with immigration, Mexican drug cartels, and wildfires, yet she continues to battle the federal government on states' rights issues.

Title IX

Title IX of the Education Amendment of 1972 mandated that schools not deny any student participation in any educational program or activity on the basis of sex. Now we all know that Oklahoma University is not going to build a football stadium for girls the size of the one they have for boys. But there are still some gender equity issues that remain:

- Girls at risk of dropping out of school
- Gender bias in student/teacher interactions
- Date rape
- Gender bias in standardized tests
- Teen pregnancy and parenting
- Sexual harassment of students by their peers
- The participation and achievement of girls in math and science.

Abortion

This is a major issue for women. The legal and moral aspects of it will be debated for the rest of my life, I'm sure. And while some would argue that fathers should have a voice in any abortion decision, the pregnancy, delivery, and postnatal care for the child belong uniquely to the woman. I am a pro-life guy, no two ways about it. But I sympathize with families whose daughters get pregnant because they were raped.

Abuse

My wife does some work at a battered women's shelter, and the stories she hears would break your heart. Of all the women murdered in the United States, about one-third are killed by a spouse or boyfriend. The leading cause of death for pregnant women is murder by a partner. It is estimated that in 2008, more than one million American women were raped.[59] There can be no doubt that misogyny exists in America.

Degradation

Pornography in the United States, or anywhere for that matter, simply degrades woman. They are exploited and abused.

International

Part of the reason women in America struggle for gender equality is because internationally, other women have it much worse. Below are some of the common practices in the Middle East:[56]

- In Saudi Arabia, women are not allowed to drive.
- In Lebanon, battered women cannot file for divorce without an eyewitness to the abuse.
- In Afghanistan, girls quit school when they reach puberty.
- In Egypt, women cannot travel abroad without permission.
- In many countries in the region, there are no laws to punish perpetrators of domestic violence.
- Muslim women are required to meet a dress code or risk attack, and they have no voice in family decision making.
- In Bahrain, judges can deny women custody of their children for arbitrary reasons.
- In Morocco, courts strongly favor men over women in adultery cases.
- In many countries in the region, only fathers can pass citizenship to their children.
- In Iraq, women in the military are more likely to be raped by a fellow soldier than killed by the enemy.

These types of situations are almost unthinkable in America.

In America

Women in the United States seem to believe, even as little girls, that their appearance is the dominant success factor in their life. Men achieve. Women have to look good and then achieve. Women seem conditioned by society that the preferred and expected progression in their lives is to marry and have children. Careers and achievements are tertiary. Because we seem to value *pretty* more than anything else in little girls, they come to learn that. Consequently, little girls put that law on their lens. We don't seem to do that with little boys.

As a result, and it's no surprise, many young girls develop another law that says, "My self-worth directly correlates to how pretty I am. And if boys aren't attracted to me, then I must not be pretty." With that law on a girl's lens, what do you think she will do when the captain of the football team asks her out and then wants to have sex with her? Of course she'll sleep with him. Her whole self-worth is tied up in it! Ladies, your self-worth is not tied in any way to how people rate your appearance.

We need to change that law. Nothing external decides your value or self-worth. Only you can decide that, so don't let anyone else take that from you. You, young lady, are of great value! Don't ever forget that.

Conclusion

Have you ever heard someone say, "What do you expect, she's a girl?" If so, then you know a law that is on his lens. How do think a father with that law will treat his daughter, his wife, his sister, or his female employees? How many dumb blond jokes have you ever heard that were about a man? We are just conditioned to a double standard in so many subliminal ways.

There once was a man driving his son to the boy's Little League baseball game. At an intersection, they were hit by another car when a drunk driver ran a stop light. The father had minor injuries, but the boy was bleeding and unconscious. Paramedics arrived and took both the father and his son to the emergency room at the hospital. The young boy was placed in a treatment room with curtains drawn around him. The father was sitting beside his son holding his hand and praying. Finally, the doctor came in, looked down at the little boy, and said, "My God, that's my son!" Who is the doctor?

Go on, guess. Don't worry, I didn't get it either the first time I heard it.

It is the boy's mother! We are subliminally conditioned to believe that certain occupations are exclusively male and others are exclusively female. It's not that you mean to, but subconsciously you put laws on your lens that say, "Doctors are men." The above story proves it.

We tend to see things that match the laws on our lenses. Most of us have laws that tell us that hearts and diamonds are red and spades and clubs are black. But what if somebody showed you a black diamond or a red club? It would take you a moment, because you're trying to see the cards *the right way*, according to the laws on your lens. The laws about the colors of card suits filter what you actually see, tricking you into seeing what you think you're supposed to see—black clubs and red diamonds. Doctors are supposed to be men, so that's what we think, and sometimes that's what we actually see. Perhaps we do the same with attorneys, and football players, and presidents, and first-grade teachers. We actually have laws on our lenses about everything, not just occupations.

As long as men and women remain different, we will probably never experience pure and true gender equality. Men are from Mars and women are from Venus, right? We're definitely anatomically different, and perhaps we should celebrate our differences rather than try to make everything equal. Fairness would be a better measure. I'm a believer in fairness. And women in America today are not getting a fair shake.

27

The *PLEASE CHANGE YOUR MIND* Process

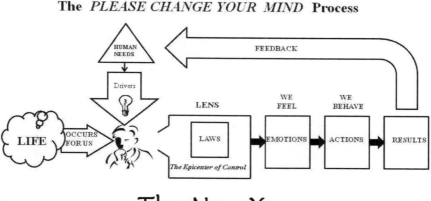

The New You

The diagram above shows that life occurs for you at one hundred miles per hour every day. At the same time, you have a set of five basic human needs that you're trying to meet for yourself. In addition, you have a lens through which you filter life as it occurs for you. You process everything through this lens. On this lens you have placed laws that you hold to be true. These laws cover every aspect of your life. The chapter titles in this book are just some of the many aspects of your life; there are hundreds more. You have laws about loading the dishwasher, personal safety, marriage, raising children, governmental policy, cutting the grass—everything!

So every time something happens (you see something, you hear something, you taste something, etc.), the first thing you do is process it through your lens. Then, based on your laws, you *think* something. It happens in this sequence every time. So if you have a law on your lens that says "All snakes are dangerous," then that is what you will think every time you see a snake. If you have a law on your lens that says, "My parents don't love me," then anything and everything they ever do will be processed and interpreted by you as not emanating from love, but from some other motivation. Every time!

Based on what you think, you will then feel something. In the case of snakes, you will probably feel fear. In the case of your parents, you may feel skepticism, insincerity, or doubt. But you will feel something. These feelings will then dictate your behavior, or what you do. You have no choice. Your behavior is programmed, based on the laws on your lens. Your behavior is predictable. So focusing on behavior modification will only give you a short-term improvement. You have to change the law on your lens to create permanent behavior modification.

Your behavior then creates results in your life. In the case of snakes, you will always feel fear, you will always run away, and the results will be that you will never be bitten by a snake. In the case of your parents, you will always feel skeptical or doubtful, you will always respond accordingly, and the results will be that you won't have the best relationship with your parents.

You then have to ask yourself, "Are these results meeting my needs?" In the case of snakes, you'd have to say that your results are meeting your needs, given that you've never been bitten by a snake. But in the case of your parents, maybe your results aren't meeting your needs. Maybe you'd like to have a better relationship with your parents. So change the law on your lens to say, "Maybe my parents love me," or "My parents do love me." You have the power to do that. In fact, since you can't control your parents' feelings or behavior, the only thing you can do, the only thing you have control over, is changing the law on your lens. Do that and then see what kind of results that creates for you.

In the end, it doesn't really matter whether your parents love you or not. What matters is whether or not you *think* they do. What you think drives everything else. And the only person who controls what you think is *you*. It doesn't matter what your parents do or don't do. You're not in control of that anyway. If you think they love you, then you will see everything from that perspective. If you think they don't love you, then you will see everything from that perspective. Each perspective will drive a different behavior, and that behavior will create different results. One is more likely to meet your needs than the other. And always remember that results take time to measure.

Now I'm not trying to tell you that the laws on your lens are good or bad, or right or wrong. I'm just telling you that you have a lens, and that you have laws on that lens. Those laws are driving what you feel and how you behave, and that is creating the results in your life. If those results aren't meeting your needs over time, it probably means you have a law that should be examined. The process of taking laws off your lens, examining them, changing them, and creating better results for yourself is the basis of all human growth. The good news is that you are in total control of those laws and what you think.

The *Please Change Your Mind* diagram is also useful in observing other people. If you see a repeated behavior in someone, you can begin to guess which of the five human needs is probably driving that behavior. Based on that need, you can try to guess the possible laws on the person's lens that might be driving his or her emotions and behavior. If you are able to do that, then predicting the person's future behavior becomes relatively easy. If that same person is familiar with the language of the diagram, then you can have a discussion with him or her about your observations. Instead of approaching him or her in a critical way about his or her behavior, you can approach him or her in a constructive way and discuss the laws on his or her lens, not his or her behavior. This is a powerful tool for families when everyone understands the diagram and uses the language.

There is a poem about what trees think. I do not know the author, but it has great applicability for all of us.

TREES

I am not sure what trees think,
Since they don't put them down in ink,
But clearly they are not the kind,
That jog and jostle in my mind.

Trees live with such gentle ease,
I wish that I could think like trees,
I wish that like a tree I might,
Grow always, only toward the light.

And had no need to run about
the world, to seek my meaning out.

But if I could think like a tree,
I wonder if I could not see,
My meaning comes from being me.

The essential thing is to think. Thoughts control everything, even for trees. Your meaning comes from being you—and the way you think.

So in the end, you *are* what you *think*. And what you *think* is all in your *mind*. You have total control. You need no one's permission to change. So if the results you're creating aren't meeting your needs—Please Change Your Mind.

Acknowledgments

As with all books, authors have many people to thank. I'm no different. Thanks to Vicki Willard, who was the first person to tell me I should write this book. I would also like to thank John Boushell for his early editorial work.

I would like to thank all the people at iUniverse, most of whom I haven't even met yet. I want to thank them in advance for getting my book on the *New York Times* bestseller list and for getting me appearances on both Letterman and Dr. Phil. Just kidding. But I know they'll do their best!

And lastly, I'd like to thank my wife, Sherrie, for all her support throughout this process. Hats are off also to our wonderful children, who allowed me to write about them and share our experiences with you.

About the Author

Steve White was a partner at Arthur Young and the founder of several management consulting firms. Currently, he helps companies develop strategic plans, and he writes books. Retired, White lives in Atlanta, Georgia, with his wife, Sherrie, and their cat, Cashmere.

Chapter Notes

The *Please Change Your Mind* process diagram was developed by Steve White to make it easier for readers to follow the manuscript.

Chapter 1

    1 – "Abraham Maslow's Hierarchy of Needs," http://en.wikipedia.org/wiki/maslow's_hierchy_of_needs.

Chapter 2

    2 – "Old Woman, Young Woman," http://mathworld.wolfram.com/YoungGirl-OldWomanillusion. html.

Chapter 3

    3 – Diagram used by doctors during my in-patient counseling.

Chapter 5

    4 – Lance Bezel, "Three Generations of Springs Family Accused in Welfare Fraud," *Denver Post*, January 12, 2011, http://www.denverpost.com/news/ci_17076085.

Chapter 8

5 – "Major Religions of the World Ranked by Number of Adherents,"
http://www.adherents.com/Religions_By_Adherents.html.

Chapter 10

6 – Jiaquan Xu, MD, Kenneth D. Kochanek, MA, Sherry L.
Murphy, BS, and Betzaida Tejada-Vera, BS, "Deaths: Final Data
for 2007," *National Vital Statistics Report* 58, no. 19, (May 20,
2010), http://www.cdc.gov/nchs/data/nvsr/nvsr58_19.pdf.

7 – "The Top 10 Leading Causes of Death in America," WEGO
Health, http://community.wegohealth.com/profiles/blogs/the
-top-10-leading-causes-of-death.

8 – Amanda Gardner, "Many Americans Don't Even Know They're
Fat," Health.com, http://news.health.com/2010/09/02/many
-americans-dont-even-know-theyre-fat/.

9 – Ibid.

10 – "Lung Cancer," Cancer.Net Editorial Board, last modified
February 18, 2011, accessed May 3, 2011, http://www.cancer.net
/patient/Cancer+Types/Lung+Cancer?sectionTitle=Statistics.

11 – "Worldwide HIV & AIDS Statistics," accessed May 2, 2011,
http://www.avert.org/worldstats.htm.

12 – "Worldwide HIV & AIDS Statistics," accessed May 2, 2011,
http://www.avert.org/worldstats.htm.

13 – United States HIV & AIDS Statistics Summary," accessed May
2, 2011, http://www.avert.org/usa-statistics.htm.

Chapter 13

14 –Gardiner Harris, "Out-of-Wedlock Birthrates Are Soaring, U.S. Reports," *New York Times*, May 13, 2009, http://www.nytimes.com/2009/05/13/health/13mothers.html.

15 – Wayne Parker, "Statistics on Fatherless Children in America," http://fatherhood.about.com/od/fathersrights/a/fatherless_children.htm.

"Fathers Unite," accessed September 13, 2011, http://www.fathersunite.org/statistics_on_fatherlessness.html.

"National Fatherhood Initiative," accessed May 3, 2011 http://wwwfatherhood.org/media/fatherhood-statistics.

Jesse Washington, "Blacks Struggle With 72% Unwed Mothers Rate," Associated Press, November 7, 2010, accessed May 10, 2011, http://www.msnbc.msn.com/id/39993685/ns/health-womens _health/t/blacks-struggle-percent-unwed-mothers-rate/.

Emily Yoffe, "…And Baby Makes Three," *Slate*, accessed September 17, 2011 http://www.slate.com/id/2185944/.

Jack Cashell, "It's the Culture, Stupid," *American Thinker*, March 14, 2010, accessed September 17, 2011, http://www.americanthinker.com/2010/03/its_the_culture_stupid.html.

16 – George Barna, *The Future of the American Family* (Chicago: Moody Publishers, 1993).

17 – I wrote this just before my daughter Jennifer's wedding.

18 – *The Bridge Builder* by Will Allen Dromgoole, published 1900.

Chapter 14

19 – www.Kiwanis.org and http://en.wikipedia.org/wiki/Kiwanis.

20 – Wikipedia, http://en.wikipedia.org/wiki/Ku_Klux_Klan.

21 – Wikipedia, http://en.wikipedia.org/wiki/Rotary_International.

22 – Steve Nawajczyk Group, copyright 1997, accessed May15, 2011, http://www.gangwar.com/dynamics.htm.

23 – All information found on each group's website or Wikipedia.

www.lionsclubs.org or http://en.wikipedia.org/wiki/Lions_Clubs_International.

www.legion.org.

www.shrinersinternational.org or http://en.wikipedia.org/wiki /Shriners.

www.aarp.org or http://en.wikipedia.org/wiki/AARP.

www.aa.org or http://en.wikipedia.org/wiki/Alcoholis _Anonymous.

www.nra.org or http://en.wikipedia.org/wiki/National_Rifle _Association.

www.madd.org or http://en.wikipedia.org/wiki/Mothers _Against_Drunk_Driving.

www.humanesociety.org.

www.unicef.org or http://en.wikipedia.org/wiki/UNICEF.

www.marines.com or http://en.wikipedia.org/wiki/United
_States_marine_corps.

Chapter 16

24 – "News Release," Bureau of Labor Statistics, May 20, 2011,
http://www.bls.gov/news.release/archives/laus_05202011.pdf.

25 – Dina ElBoghdady and Nancy Trejos, "Foreclosure Rate Hits
Historic High," *Washington Post*, June 15, 2007,
http://www.washingtonpost.com/wp-dyn/content
/article/2007/06/14/AR2007061400513.html.

26 – "Foreclosure Statistics," NeighborWorks America,
http://www.fdic.gov/about/comein/files/foreclosures_staistics.pdf.

Chapter 17

27 – "Passenger Vehicles in the United States," last modified
September 8, 2011, http://en.wikipedia.org/wiki/Passenger
_Vehicles_in_the_United_States.

Chapter 18

28 – "Education in the United States," last modified September 14,
2011, http://en.wikipedia.org/wiki/Education_in_the_United
_States#statistics.

29 – "Fiscal Year 2011 Budget Summary – February 1, 2010," United
States Department of Education, http://www2.ed.gov/about
/overview/budget/budget11/summary/edlite-section1.html.

30 – "Trends in International Mathematics and Science Study," last modified July 6, 2011, http://en.wikipedia.org/wiki/Trends_in _International_Mathematics_and_Science_Study.

31 – Pascal Forgione, "Poor U.S. Test Results Tied to Weak Curriculum," accessed September 13, 2011, http://4brevard.com /choice/international-test-scores.htm. For additional thoughts on education in America by Pascal Forgione, visit http://thenewamerican.com/culture/education/8863-an-extreme -makeover-for-us-education-can-we-should-we.

Chapter 20

32 – Etienne Bensen, "Rehabilitate or Punish," American Psychological Association, accessed May 24, 2011, http://www.apa.org/monitor/julaug03/rehab.aspx.

33 – "10 Stats You Should Know about Our Prison System," Criminal Justice USA, May 17, 2011, http://www.criminaljusticeusa/blog/2011/10-stats-you-should -know-about-out-prison-system.

34 – "Poll: Infidelity Is Common Knowledge in the USA," *USA Today*, accessed May 24, 2011, http://abcnews.go.com/Health/Sex/story?id=4480097&page=1.

35 – "Infidelity Statistics," copyright 2006, accessed May 24, 2011, http://infidelityfacts.com/infidelity-statistics.html.

36 –"Divorce Rate in America," accessed May 24, 2011, http://www.divorcerate.com.

37 – Jill Grayson, "Cohabitation Numbers Jump 13%, Linked to Job Losses," *USA Today*, January 27, 2011,

http://www.usatoday.com/news/nation/census/2010-09-24
-cohabitation24ONLINE_ST_N.htm.

38 – "Impact of Drugs on Society," U.S. Department of Justice
National Drug Intelligence Center 2010, accessed May 24, 2011,
http://www.justice.gov/ndic/pubs38/38661/drugImpact.htm.

39 – Jennifer Warren, "Premarital Sex the Norm in America,"
WebMD, December 20, 2006, http://webmd.com
/sexrelationships/news/20061220/premarital-se-the-norm-in
-america.

40 – Jackie Wold, "An Overview on the Evolution of Sex in America
– Its Effects on Future Families," Spring 2010, accessed May 24,
2011, http://stthomas.edu/familystudies/pdf/student-papers
-spring2011/Evolution%20of%20Sex%20in%20.pdf.

41 – "Poll: More Profanity in America," ABC News, March 29,
2006, accessed May 24, 2011, http://abclocal.go.com/wpvi
/story?section=news/national_world&id+4034648.

42 – "Profanity," Wikipedia, accessed May 24,2011,
http://en.wikipedia.org/wiki/Profanity.

43 – Jerry Ropelata, "Internet Pornography Statistics," Top 10
Reviews, accessed May 24, 2011, http://internet-filter-review
.toptenreviews.com/internet-pornography-statistics.html.

"Statistics on Pornography, Sexual Addiction and Online
Perpetrators," TechMission Corps, accessed May 24, 2011,
http://www.safefamilies.org/sfStats.php.

"Possible Harmful Effects of Pornography in Society," accessed
May 24, 2011, http://yeeha.org/enterhtml/live/Dark/porn.html.

44 – Randall K. Bannon, PhD, "Fifty Million Lost Lives Since 1973,"
National Right to Life News, January 2008, accessed September
16, 2011, http://www.nrlc.org/news/2008/NRL01/LiveLost.html.

45 – "2010 Josephson Institute's Report Card on Ethics in American
Youth: Part One—Integrity Summary Data," accessed September
2011, http://charactercounts.org/programs/reportcard/..

46 – "Homosexuality and Psychology," Wikipedia, accessed June 3,
2011, http://en.wikipedia.org/wiki/Homosexuality.

Chapter 22

47 – Ray Kurzweil, *The Age of Spiritual Machines* (New York: Viking
Press, 1999).

Chapter 23

48 – "Life Expectancy in the United States," CRS Reports for
Congress, last modified August 16, 2006,
http://aging.senate.gov/crs/aging1.pdf.

49 – "New Medicines Transforming Patient Care," PhRMA, accessed
September 17, 2011, http://phrma.org/new-medicines
-transforming-patient-care.

Chapter 24

50 – Charles Hall, "Ecology," Encyclopedia of Earth, accessed June
14, 2011, http://www.eoearth.org/article/Ecology.

51 – "The Role of the EPA," Eco-Evaluator, accessed June 14, 2011.
http://www.ecoevaluator.com/environment/organizations/the-
role-of-the-epa.html.

Chapter 25

52 – Toni Johnson, "Nuclear Power Safety Concerns," Council on Foreign Relations, last modified March 30, 2011, http://www.cfr.org/europerussia/nuclear-power-safty-concerns/p10534.

53 – "How Geothermal Energy Works," Union of Concerned Scientists, accessed June 14, 2011, http://ucsusa.org/clean_energy/technology_and_impacts/energy_technologies/how-geothermal-energy-works.html.

"Clean Energy," Union of Concerned Scientists, accessed September 17, 2011, http://www.ucsusa.org/clean_energy/technology_the_impacts/energy_technologies/how-geothermal_energy_works.html.

Chapter 26

54 – Jane Morse, "Women's Rights in the United States," America.gov Archives, February 26, 2007, http://www.america.gov/st/diversity-english/2007/February/20070226171718ajesrom0.636 6846.html.

55 – Margery Elfin and Sue Headlee, *The Cost of Being Female*, (Santa Barbara, CA: Praeger Publishers, 1996).

56 – "10 Extreme Examples of Gender Inequality," Listverse, November 20, 2008, http://listverse.com/2008/11/20/10-extreme-examples-of-gender-inequality.

57 – "Women in Congress," accessed September 17, 2011, http://womenincongress.house.gov/historical-data/representatives-senators-by-congress.html?congress=112.

58 – "List of Current United States Governors," Wikipedia, accessed September 17, 2011, http://en.wikipedia.org/wiki/List_of _United_States_Governors.

59 – Jessica Valenti, "For Women in America, Equality is Still an Illusion," *Washington Post*, February 28, 2010, http://www.washingtonpost.com/wp-dtn/content /article/2010/02/19/AR2010221902049.html.